A Spot at the Bar

A Spot at the Bar

Welcome to The Everleigh
The art of good drinking in three hundred recipes

hardie grant books

This was supposed to be Sasha's time to speak. Sasha Petraske, my mentor, business partner and dear friend passed away in August 2015. He was 42.

Sasha was responsible for opening the most important bar of our time. How can a bar be important, you ask? When Milk & Honey opened its doors on 31 December 1999, that little bar behind an unmarked door on Eldridge Street in New York City forever changed the way bartenders around the world made drinks.

Sasha was a pioneer, leading the way by inspiring us to make the very best drinks we could. His passion for ice enabled each of us to understand its relevance and importance, and he taught us that working hard behind the scenes allows you to look effortless in front of your guests. He'd tell you himself he wasn't the first, or the only. He just cared, and he put his money where his mouth was – all of it.

Sasha was a visionary in every sense. He loved the industry, the business, the drinks and his staff. He gave the industry a lot more than he ever took out. As for his customers, he loved them dearly. He was loyal to his regulars and never forgot who put him where he was.

Sasha had a terrible memory. The third time we met he apologised and said he was 'like a goldfish man. Every time around the bowl is like the first time.' He once left his bike chained up in Union Square and totally forgot where he'd left it until a year later, when he came into Milk & Honey with it one night.

He was the most intimidating man I've ever known. He didn't yell at you, ever. Instead he spoke very quietly when he was disappointed. No one wanted to disappoint Sasha. Don't get me wrong, there were times I wanted to beat him with a muddler for interrupting me while I was ten tickets deep on a Saturday night, but he didn't have an ego. He was just Sasha.

When Sasha came off the bar, it was the right thing to do. He had a dream. He was bigger than the bar. He had a responsibility to this industry. You had to earn your seat next to Sasha and I'm glad that I earnt mine. I would have rolled under a bus for him and his cause and I'm not the only one. For a cocktail cause, you ask? Yep, absolutely. Reading this back, it sounds a little like he was a cult leader, but whatever – I drank the Kool-Aid. I was in hook, line and sinker and what a quest it felt like, to follow someone who believed in something so passionately, to be part of something special, something bigger than yourself. This was certainly a great honour, but not as great as opening my first bar, The Everleigh, with Sasha at my side. Having Sasha as my business partner and having a bar of my own, thanks to him, thanks to all he had already given me. All I wanted to do was make him proud.

I carry a lot of Sasha in me today – some good, some bad. He didn't look to make a name for himself; he didn't want fame. He wanted a perfect bar with perfect drinks. He wanted the perfect bartenders and perfect servers for his perfect service. He wanted perfection. He wasn't perfect, he knew that, but his pursuit was.

The last time I saw Sasha was about eight weeks before he died. We'd met up in London. I was excited about starting the build on my second Melbourne bar, Heartbreaker; he was excited about the new projects he had lined up for the year.

We talked about the Heartbreaker project and his eyes lit up. He loved new starts. It was like telling your father about a new toy or school project. We finished our drinks and I got the bill, as always. I walked him to his cab. We hugged and he got in the car. In true Sasha fashion, he didn't turn to wave or say goodbye, he just looked straight ahead and the car drove away. I thought, you classy bastard.

He'd love this book. I'm really happy to say that.

Here's to you, Chief. Thank you for your weirdness, and your tireless devotion to your staff. You are loved, you are missed, and you will always be remembered.

May the force be with you.

Mr Madrusan

Photo by Daniel Krieger

'A cocktail waits for no man.'

– Sasha Petraske

INTRODUCTION

I opened The Everleigh on 4 July 2011 with empty pockets and high expectations. The pressure involved in opening the newest addition to New York City's Milk & Honey family was enormous, and the honour even greater.

We built The Everleigh together, as a family, with blood, sweat, tears and whiskey – so much whiskey. My parents lent me the money, my sister designed the bar, and my childhood friend managed the build.

Entering The Everleigh is a singular Melbourne experience. Come in through the corner door of a diner, walk down a hallway and climb a few stairs and be whisked back in time to a classic cocktail bar of the golden era. My aim was to make people feel the way I felt every time I walked through the curtains at Milk & Honey. I wanted to recreate that mystery and awe, to build anticipation and excitement about the evening ahead and then, ultimately, to live up to that expectation, every time.

When you sit down it feels nice, right? My mother upholstered the leather seats and we even handmade the buttons. That personal, family touch is ever present. We kept a photo log on our social media page – they're all there! Those tired but happy faces, pulling together for a common goal. Ten weeks' work for a lifetime of memories.

In June 2013 we did it all again to create The Elk Room, tucked away inside The Everleigh, and then once more in August 2015 for Heartbreaker. It's been a long road. I've seen bright days, and I've seen dark days when we have fought to stay open. Those times have tested me beyond words but, five years on, she's still there, my beautiful Everleigh. Every time I walk into that bar I fall in love all over again. I am truly grateful to everyone, near and far, who has helped me along the way.

The Everleigh was designed to deliver detail-oriented, attentive service. The entire operation is focused upon your experience, and our skill lies in making it a great one. No standing in queues, no waiting at the bar to get served, no missing time with your friends because it's your round. No inconsistency when it comes to drinks. No mixologists, no ego, just selfless service, seven nights a week.

What sets us apart is the fact that we want to get to know you. We spend time with each guest to ensure that their experience is entirely interactive and engaging. We suggest that anyone who's after a cocktail opt for Bartender's Choice, leaving it to us to deliver exactly what they're after. The Everleigh team is a very close, hard-working little family, all dedicated to the same goal. We don't take ourselves too seriously (you'll see that as you journey through this book) but we're incredibly proud to be part of this industry – to be part of a global family – and we're proud to serve you.

A Spot at the Bar is an invitation. No matter where you're sitting, an evening at The Everleigh is an intimate encounter. We see every seat in the bar as an opportunity to have a new and exciting experience. While you're there, we want you to own it, and when you leave, we want you to remember it.

By capturing what is so special about The Everleigh, we hope to extend this experience into your home. To let you take everything that made your evening memorable, and have it inspire the next.

Like the bar itself, this book pays a lot of attention to service. Our dedication to method and technique ensures consistency and reduces the variables. The bartender should be making perfect drinks – every drink that comes across the bar should be delicious. Take this as assumed; we don't need to harp on it. We're more interested in the elements that you can be involved in, more interested in getting to know our customers and forming relationships with our loyal regulars.

We welcome you with a loud hello and a big smile. We hand write our bills with a 'thank you' on the back. We even have Everleigh postcards and a mailbox by the door so our guests can send a little love to someone anywhere in the world. We're about bringing people closer. We're about the good times. We're excited about what we can learn from each new encounter, and we want you to be too.

This book is a journey from the beginning of your evening to the morning after. We start by taking you behind the bar, handing over all our tools and showing you the ropes. This will set you up for the fun stuff to come. There's a lot more to this book than just cocktail recipes. That said, we've used the holy grail, our Cocktail Branches, to provide over three hundred drinks! We didn't invent them all – this book is a collection of our favourite cocktails, classic and modern, and, most of all, the drinks our guests come back for.

We're not the only ones who hold The Everleigh dear and we're truly honoured to have played a part in so many magical moments over the years, from birthdays and engagements to full-blown wedding ceremonies!

For all those who love The Everleigh, all those we're so proud to serve, we made a book for you.

So then, a spot at the bar? Absolutely, take a seat. Let's get started.

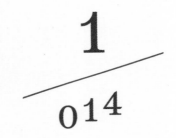

$$\frac{1}{014}$$

Tools of the Trade

When putting this book together, we left this chapter until the end – funny, seeing as you need it to begin. When we started writing we really wanted to make sure it wouldn't be 'another boring bar book' or referred to simply as a 'cocktail recipe book'. By the end of the writing process we revelled in getting down to the crux of what we do, what we use and each item's specific importance.

As much as we endeavoured to make this more than 'just a cocktail book', we have to accept that we do take cocktails incredibly seriously. In fact, we wouldn't have had the chance to write this book if we didn't. Our drinks are far from complicated, and there is no smoke and mirrors in regard to how we make or serve them. It's our methodical approach to making drinks, paired with a strong understanding of balance and flavour, that grants us some authority in the field.

You don't need all the bells and whistles to make perfect drinks. Function and practicality are paramount to the way we do things. As a result, everything in The Everleigh has a purpose, a role and a reason. We leave nothing to chance.

In this chapter we've listed all our essential bits and bobs and explained how to use them. Shakers, jiggers, strainers – it's nothing you haven't seen before. We're definitely not mathematicians, but we did crunch some serious numbers to get everything perfect.

Enough chat; let's get down to business.

ICE

What's in your drink? At The Everleigh we used to freeze, rotate and hand-cut all our own ice before every shift. This process took almost two hours, and no one was exempt from the task. In January 2015, after five years of this labour-intensive, home-style operation (I'd had another five years of this in New York too!) we gathered up the bank loans and the audacity to open our own ice company, Navy Strength Ice. We bought some huge ice block–making machines that look remarkably like coffins, known as Clinebells, and began our quest to offer Melbourne perfect, crystal clear, hand-cut ice blocks to put in their drinks. By slowly freezing purified water fed through our state of the art filtration system, these machines are able to produce a 150-kg block of ice every three days, every inch of which is crystal clear. We then cut these down with various oversized Japanese ice saws and tools to craft cubes and spears that are the perfect size for our Negronis and Tom Collins'.

Ice is broadly acknowledged as one of the most important ingredients in mixed drinks, yet somehow this component still seems to get overlooked. Ice is so important, because it is the only cocktail ingredient with a specific

job to do. While its primary function is to chill the drink, it is also crucial for adding dilution, and this dilution is difficult to control. For example, when using small pieces of inferior ice in drinks such as a Negroni or an Old Fashioned, the ice will begin to melt before the drink has even left the bar. Ever noticed a film-like layer of water appearing on top of your rocks drink soon after you began drinking it? Sure you have, and this poor-quality water and excess dilution is guaranteed to interfere with the taste of the cocktail. The alternative is clear. By using large, dense, purified blocks of ice we are able to chill the drink quickly without diluting it, ensuring the last sip is as delicious as the first.

The same principles apply to shaking cocktails. At The Everleigh we don't just use our fancy ice in drinks that will show it off, we also shake with it. Shaking cocktails with hard, clear block ice allows us to completely control the dilution of a drink. Essentially, the purpose of shaking a drink is to both 'awaken' and combine each of the ingredients while also chilling them and adding the desired amount of water. As the drink and the ice are agitated, the large, dense block moves back and forth in the shaker, cooling the drink without shattering into smaller pieces that would begin to dilute too quickly. A cocktail shaken with clear block ice is perfectly cold, light and fluffy, with a foamy head formed from the finest ice crystals. Now, who's thirsty?

As we've mentioned, ice is a fickle mistress with a number of variables. For this reason, we've included a quick care and handling guide, courtesy of team Navy Strength, to help you get the best out of your blocks and your drinks!

Care & handling

01 Ice is a food product. Only touch it with clean hands.

02 Ice has the ability to both absorb and release aroma and flavour. If you're planning to store your ice in a freezer with other food items, ensure that your ice is kept in sealed bags or containers.

03 Store your ice in a temperature-controlled freezer at all times in order to maintain its shape and clarity and to prevent melting and bonding.

04 Before handling, ensure that your ice is not too cold. If the ice is too cold it will crack easily when handled. To avoid this, it is best to remove your ice from the freezer a little in advance and allow it to climb slightly in temperature for a minute or so before handling.

05 Upon serving, be sure to coat your ice block with liquid to remove the frost. If your ice is of premium quality, this will make it look clean and clear.

06 For cocktails on the rocks, be sure to either build your rocks drink first in your round – if you're making more than one drink – or else give it a few spins before serving. A drink served on a block of ice is less delicate than any others, therefore it can technically wait for the other drinks and will actually benefit from the dilution provided by sitting on a rock for a minute or two. Remember, this is a hard, dense block and it will therefore dilute very slowly. A cocktail served over a block is not intended to be diluted at first, however this piece of ice will ensure the drink maintains its integrity until the last sip.

Types of ice

Blocks We use large crystal clear blocks for all 'rocks' drinks – those intended to be served over a large piece of ice.

As explained, the dense block does away with the watery Negroni that tasted great two minutes ago. It slows the dilution right down. Did we mention you can also read a book through it?

Cracked This is just our block ice cracked down, or smashed into pieces half the size of store-bought ice.

We crack ice behind the bar prior to making stirred drinks such as Manhattans and Martinis. The smaller pieces of ice allow us to bring the drink down to temperature as we stir. As soon as these drinks reach the ideal temperature and dilution, the liquid is strained into the glass and the ice is discarded.

Cracked ice also features in cocktails such as our Gordon's Cup *(see page 98)*. In this case, we muddle the fruit, add the spirits, then add cracked ice before tossing the drink briefly and emptying it into a frozen double rocks glass.

Crushed This is ice crushed down into small, pellet-like ice chips, perfect for citrusy drinks in summertime.

When making mixed drinks with crushed ice, note that the volume of each cube is very small, therefore it is going to melt and settle quickly. To slow this process, add your drink to a frozen glass before adding your crushed ice. Swizzle briefly and then top up the ice as it will have settled into the glass. Always ensure a good mound of ice sits on top of the drink before serving.

Crushed ice is ideal for use when whipping drinks *(see page 31)*. Adding a small handful of pellets to the shaker will aerate the ingredients without fear of overdiluting. This ice is also used for fixes such as the Bramble *(see page 117)* and the Queen's Park Swizzle *(see page 110)*.

Shaking We shake all our drinks with large blocks as described previously, allowing us to fully control dilution. This is particularly important in the case of delicate citrus drinks served without ice, such as Daiquiris, which start to decompose the moment you stop shaking.

Spears These are long, spear-like pieces of ice that go into all our tall drinks. Dubbed 'magic ice' by our customers – this stuff is so clear that if it's in your gin and tonic you can't even see it!

GLASSWARE

Beer / pilsner glass Whatever your preference – just make sure they fit the whole beer, which will be approximately 360 ml (12 fl oz). Keep this one chilled in the fridge.

Cocktail glass (aka Champagne saucer, coupe or coupette) We use various cocktail glasses in the bar, the rule being that they must be no smaller than 165 ml (5½ fl oz) and no larger than 195 ml (6½ fl oz).

I really love a Nick and Nora glass. This is a glass with a tall stem and small, round chalice, so very classy. We use these for stirred cocktails, and wide, shorter-stemmed glasses for our shaken cocktails.

Smaller-style cocktail glasses are our favourite for flips, though you really can use whatever you like. Raid vintage markets or your grandparents' liquor cabinets and you're bound to find something special.

All cocktail glasses should be kept frozen. However, we do also keep some saucers aside at room temperature for Champagne, served the classy way.

Collins / highball glass For all your tall and refreshing drinks. We use a 360 ml (12 fl oz) glass and add a tall ice spear that leaves room for an approx. 60 ml (2 fl oz) top up of soda or such. Must be kept frozen.

Double rocks glass The double rocks glass is a wide, short tumbler. Try to find one with a heavy base, to add weight to the drink. We use a 400 ml (13½ fl oz) glass and our liquid is normally around the 210 ml (7 fl oz) mark, leaving a good amount of room for a big block of ice that will keep the drink very cold without diluting too quickly. Must be kept frozen.

Fizz glass Try to find a slender glass, approx. 270 ml (9 fl oz) in size. Must be kept frozen.

Julep cup You can find these online. Silver or pewter ones are great, especially when they get a patina. Don't polish them! They look great with a little wear and tear. If you don't have one, a rocks glass will do just fine.

Keep this one in the freezer so it's nice and frosty, keeping the crushed ice from melting too fast.

Rocks glass We use a beautiful 270 ml (9 fl oz) crystal rocks glass from the Czech Republic. Go on, splash out on this glass. It's for your Negronis and Old Fashioneds.

Store at room temperature, and don't forget to polish!

Sazerac glass How good must a drink be to have its own glass? We use the prettiest small liqueur glasses we can find – approx. 120 ml (4 fl oz). Store at room temperature but fill with crushed ice before making your Sazerac to lightly chill the glass (see page 126).

Shot Oh yes, please. Thought you'd never ask.

Sour glass This should be slightly larger than your coupe to allow for the added ingredient, egg! Small wine goblets are ideal, approx. 195–210 ml (6½–7 fl oz) in size. Must be kept frozen.

Toddy glass Be sure to check this one is fully heat resistant.

Wine glass Your call, boss. Whatever you like.

Chilled glassware

This is a no-brainer. Why work so hard to make a perfect cocktail and then pour it into a warm glass? Start with chilled glassware and you'll have a colder drink that will stay colder for longer.

The golden rules…

01 In some instances, frozen is paramount. Where room temperature or chilled glassware will do, we've noted this in the method.

02 Wine and Champagne are always served in room-temperature glasses.

03 Champagne cocktails are served in chilled glasses. Not frozen, but cold.

04 If there's no room for your glassware in the freezer, just leave a little ice and cold water in the glass for a few minutes in preparation.

05 Glassware should always be clean. Glassware that's not frozen should always be polished.

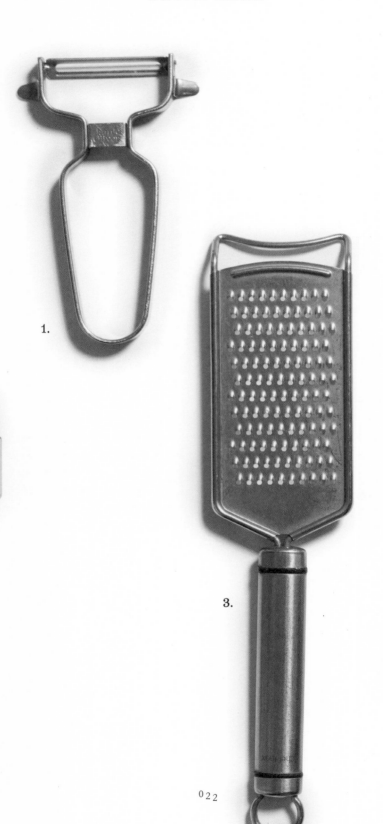

1.

2.

3.

4.

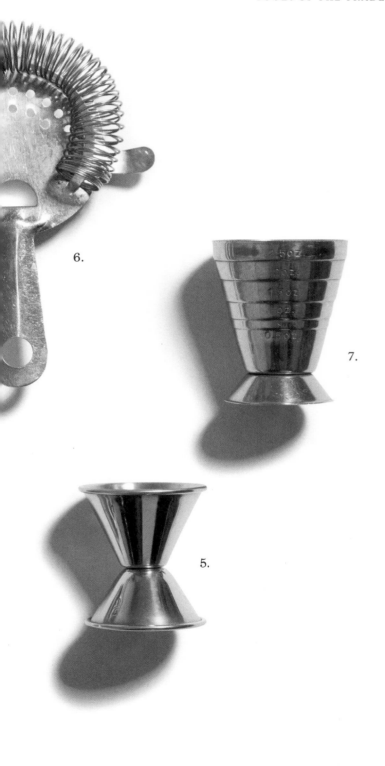

6.

7.

5.

8.

9.

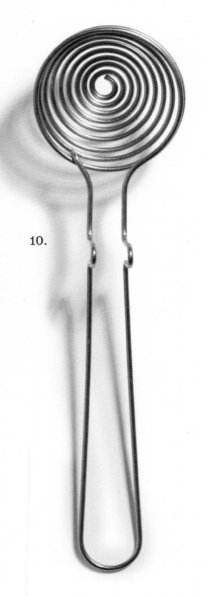

10.

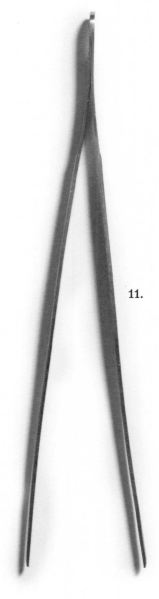

11.

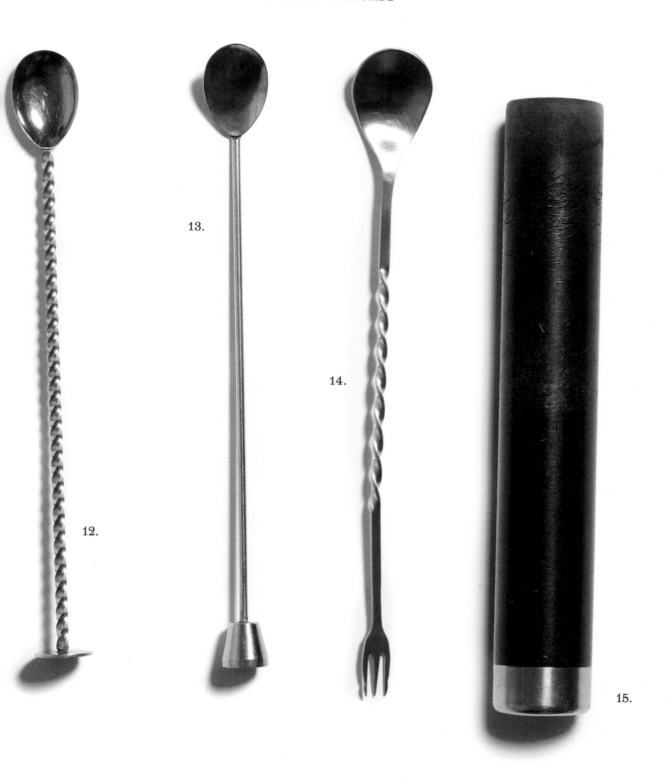

12.

13.

14.

15.

TOOLS

Here is a list of tools we use behind the bar at The Everleigh. Some we like simply because we've been using them for years, and some are particularly handy and efficient.

You don't need exactly what we have – use whatever you're comfortable with or can get your hands on.

Bar spoon / Swizzle spoon Bonzer from the UK makes a great bar spoon with a turned and twisted stem for swizzling. It has a disc on one end for crushing sugar cubes or layering, and the perfect-size bar spoon on the other end for recipes that specify a bar spoon measurement.

Bitters bottles These are dasher bottles that, when shaken, release an accurate bitters 'dash', approximately four drops of liquid. Bitters bottles are perfect when precise amounts of small-volume ingredients are needed. We use them for bitters, absinthe, orange blossom water, rosewater, peated whisky and mezcal.

Cracking spoon Our 'cracking' spoon is a long tool with a heavy spoon on the end. Hold it towards the end and crack the spoon against the flat surface of a block of ice to shatter it into numerous pieces in one fell swoop!

Cutting board Always keep one close for preparing garnishes etc. We use thin plastic food-safe boards that can be thrown away when they start to wear. Don't double up with the one you use to chop onions and garlic for dinner, as the flavour will carry. Be sure to keep it clean.

Egg separator These are great for separating the egg whites from the yolks without getting messy.

Hawthorne strainer That's the real name for the weird Y-shaped thing with bunny ears and a spring. Place it over the top of your shaker to strain a shaken cocktail into a frozen glass. There's also a finger tab there that allows you to control the flow through what we call the 'gate'.

In order to successfully hold back the seeds, chunks of ice and fruit flesh, be sure to keep the 'gate' closed from the two holes above. This allows only the liquid to pass through, giving you a cleaner, foamy head.

This method also works perfectly for pouring two cocktails at once.

Try to find Hawthornes with good, tight springs. The tighter the coil, the less mint, ice shards and fruit bits fall into the drink. You can even combine two springs for a tighter coil.

Ice crusher When I opened The Everleigh, I spent my whole bank balance on my crushed ice machine. I love her dearly.

At home, I use a little crusher from the fifties with a handle that churns the ice into smaller pieces. I bought it on eBay – there are millions available online.

No crusher? No problem. Grab a clean tea towel and a mallet and do it the old-fashioned way.

Ice pick We use this to break up or shape ice blocks when needed. They're sharp when new.

Jigger Ounces, mls, centilitres – use what you like, as long as you're using one! We always measure our ingredients to make sure we're providing a consistent product, no matter the bartender, no matter the day.

We like to use a graduated jigger that measures up to 75 ml (2½ fl oz). It's great for measuring each of the ingredients in your drink in turn without having to change your jigger.

Juicer Hand-press juicers are our preference. If it has to be electric, do be gentle. Don't push down on the fruit too hard – the pith between the skin and the fruit is quite bitter. We use a domestic cold-press juicer for our ginger and pineapple. These are great at retaining all the goodness that is lost with a juice extractor.

Julep strainer This one's for stirred drinks. The scoop-shaped strainer, modelled on an old sugar sifter, fits inside the mixing glass against the ice and allows the drink to filter through.

Knife The sharper the better. Blunt knives cut fingers. Beware!

Measuring cups A 1 litre and a 3 litre are most useful, depending on the job at hand. Again, quality will prevail here. Make sure they're clear, clean and easy to read.

Microplane The perfect tool for grating nutmeg and cinnamon. Find a good quality sharp one to help you control how much you grate. Too much nutmeg will ruin the drink.

Mixing glass This is also known as a Boston shaker. We keep these guys in the freezer. The pint glass you pinched from the pub last night will also work a treat.

Muddler I've used everything from the back of a spoon to a wooden fishing caster to muddle. Essentially, as long as it's clean you can decide what works for you. Muddlers are readily available in timber and food-safe nylon.

Peeler The Swiss or potato peeler, as they are most commonly known, is what we use. A Y-shaped peeler is the best tool for long fruit twists. Be mindful not to press down on the fruit too hard to avoid gathering too much pith, as this bit of the fruit holds all the bitterness. I'll say it once, and I'll say it again, be careful. We've seen so many fingertips hacked off with peelers. Focus, go slowly and use your thumb as a guide. Press it against the fruit as you peel so your hand doesn't fly off.

Scales Opt for digital scales for total accuracy.

Shaker The Everleigh shakers are weighted 18 oz (aka baby giant) on weighted 28 oz stainless tins. It's important to rinse your shakers in hot water between drinks. For drinks with egg products, or savoury drinks with chilli sauce, be sure to wash your shakers with soap before reusing.

We really like 'tin on tin' shakers. The classic three-piece cobbler is not really our thing and Boston shakers (mixing glass and shaker tin) are a little risky in fast-paced situations.

Stirring spoon We use a ball end stirring spoon, boasting a smooth stem for effortless stirring as the spoon is angled inwards. I also really like using plastic chopsticks to stir drinks, so we always have a stash of these behind the bar too.

Tongs These are ideal for placing in cherries and olives without splashing.

METHODS & TECHNIQUES

An explanation of terms ...

Build Adding ingredients to a glass, mixing glass or shaker. Add ice last to control dilution.

When building a drink on the rocks, add your ingredients first and then add your ice. Be sure to give the glass a few spins before serving, to chill it.

When building a crushed ice drink, add your ingredients first, then add your crushed ice. After a moment, the ice will settle into the glass, so be sure to top up the crushed ice until it forms a mound before serving.

Muddle Using a muddler or similar tool, press ingredients firmly with your palm at the back of the muddler to fully crush and extract citrus. The muddling of ingredients should be done in a shaker only – do not attempt this in a glass.

Pour Emptying all ingredients from a shaker into the glass. Not too fast. Nice and easy.

Press Using your muddler, push down lightly on the ingredients to bruise, but not fully crush.

Rinse Pouring a small amount of a liquid into a glass and swirling it around before discarding. This is usually reserved for ingredients that are quite strong in flavour, in order to add to mouthfeel without interfering too much with the other flavours in the drink. The most commonly used rinse is absinthe (see Sazerac, page 126).

Strain Placing a Hawthorne strainer (see page 26) or julep strainer (see page 27) over the top of a mixing glass or shaker, and pouring ingredients into a glass or another shaker, separating any ice, fruit or solids.

Swizzle Imagine rubbing your hands together as if you were an evil genius. Now do that with a bar spoon or swizzle spoon between your palms.

To stir or to shake?

Shaking chills faster. It makes a light and airy cocktail, best enjoyed immediately. As a rule for The Everleigh, drinks with citrus are always shaken and drinks without are stirred.

Stirring takes longer to chill, but it creates a full-bodied, concentrated cocktail with no aeration. Stirred drinks will be smooth and even taste good as they warm up.

Stirring Before stirring, add your spirits to an ice-cold mixing glass, cheapest ingredients first in case of error.

Once all ingredients have been added to the glass, begin cracking your ice for stirring. To prevent splashes when adding your ice, hold your spoon against the edge of your glass and drop or place your ice onto the spoon. Lower the ice down to the bottom. Ice added this way will prevent a splash.

Stirring should be elegant. There should be a seamless flow to your technique. Unlike shaken citrusy drinks, there is no need to agitate the ingredients or create aeration.

Try to hold your spoon around the top, in between your thumb and forefinger or middle finger. Place the spoon down the bottom of the mixing glass with the back rubbing against the glass and start stirring. Watch your mixture lines rise as the ice dilutes into the drink. Taste the mixture to check the dilution and decide when it's ready. There should be about 30 ml (1 fl oz) of water for appropriate dilution with 90 ml (3 fl oz) of alcohol.

Shaking Once your ingredients have been added to your shaker, it's time to start shaking. Shake really hard. Remember to hold the shaker firmly, with one hand on each side for protection. If not sealed tightly they can come apart. You shouldn't need to shake for more than ten seconds, unless you're shaking egg drinks, which will need a little more time to chill down.

Please note, when shaking egg drinks, you'll need to shake first *without* ice (dry shake) to emulsify the egg.

Everyone has a different shake. Find one that is comfortable for you – one that will let you shake hard and produce lively looking cocktails.

We have a few different ways in which we shake cocktails depending on the style of drink and its combination of ingredients. Some only need one quick shake because they're going to sit on ice, others need to be shaken longer and harder, and some need to be shaken twice – once without ice and once with. Here's a quick explanation of the different shaking methods we use for the drinks in this book.

Dry shake Required for drinks that contain egg, dry shaking is when a drink is first shaken without ice, to emulsify the ingredients.

Shake Shaking hard with ice.

Shake hard Shaking harder and longer – used for drinks with egg or other dense ingredients.

Toss Shaking with ice very briefly (approx. 6–8 times) to mix ingredients without adding too much dilution. Most commonly used for drinks with cracked ice.

Whip Shaking fast with just a pellet or two of cracked ice to aerate ingredients. Used mostly for bucks and highballs.

Washlines & dilution

A shaken cocktail should have a foamy head. The space between that foam and the top of the glass is called the washline. Washline is a term not used and a practice not executed nearly enough. Every time you make and strain a cocktail, think about your washlines. In many ways, they're your garnish for your final presentation.

In order to create washlines, your cocktails should be calculated for the glassware you're using. Let's face it, no one likes picking up a drink that's full to the brim – you're only going to spill it! **

Washlines can separate great drinks from not-so-great drinks. Using the washline as a guide will enable you to determine correct specifications and any changes needed, enabling you to execute great drinks that look and taste the same, night after night. If there is no washline, one of the following has likely occurred: you've shaken too long; your ice has shattered, creating high water content; the ingredients were measured incorrectly; or the drink has spilled over the sides, making your glass wet and sticky.

A shaken drink that has no head looks flat, and a cocktail filled to the brim has been made incorrectly. On the flipside, a washline that is well under the rim of the glass will look short. Either way, the washline, and therefore the drink, is ruined. We've told you before, there is method in our madness!

Pay close attention to our use of certain types of glassware and its relationship with ice. Every drink must fit the glass and, consequently, the ice must fit the drink, leaving the desired amount of space for a head or a washline.

The ice required for our 'on the rocks' and tall 'highball' or 'Collins' drinks is cut based on the desired washline of the drink the ice is going into. The benefit of having our own hand-cut ice company is that we can continually monitor and consequently alter the size of the ice in relation to the drink and the chosen glass. For example, if we opt to start using a larger rocks glass, we begin producing a larger block of ice in order to ensure the washline of the drink remains the same.

No, a bigger glass doesn't mean a bigger drink, and if you have a large block of ice in your drink that doesn't mean your cocktail is any smaller than your neighbour's! Drink specifications are measured and maintained – only the service and presentation may vary.

** *The quick rule on drink volume for a 165 ml (5½ fl oz) coupe or cocktail glass is no more than 112 ml (4 fl oz) for shaken drinks and no more than 90 ml (3 fl oz) for stirred drinks.*

GARNISHES

All fruit for garnishes should be washed and stored in the fridge or on crushed ice during service.

If you've outlaid all this money and effort on your spirits and modifiers, don't spoil the drink with old or poor-looking garnishes. After all, you see the drink before you taste it.

Bitters stripe Hold your bitters bottle by the base, pointing down, over the side of the drink. Sweep the bottle across the drink a couple of times. Practice makes perfect with this one.

Cayenne pepper Shaken from a pepper shaker, so you don't go too crazy and ruin the drink.

Cherries We use morello cherries soaked in kirsch. You can use similar, or fresh ones. Don't use the bright ones filled with E–numbers, though.

Cinnamon Cinnamon quills grated fresh over drinks are a million times better than buying already ground cinnamon. Better get yourself a microplane!

Citrus twists Using a Swiss or potato peeler, peel long twists – be careful not to go too deep, or you'll peel the pith. Peel to order, not before. Be careful using this peeler on fruit, as it slips very easily and can cause nasty injuries. I use my thumb to steady the fruit so I don't peel too fast.

Crystallised ginger Spike crystallised ginger cubes on two toothpicks so you can place them on the edge of the glass.

Cucumbers Lebanese cucumbers sliced thinly into little wheels.

Ground black pepper Freshly ground black pepper from a pepper grinder gives a great aroma to the top of the drink.

Hot sauce We use both Cholula original and chipotle. Full, flavoursome hot sauce, not too heavy on the vinegar.

Lemon / lime / orange wedges Cut into 4 cm (1½ inch) wedges and discard at the end of the night.

Mint sprigs Sprigs are the 2–3 rows of leaves at the top of the stems.

For service, store them in ice water so they don't wilt. Make sure mint sprigs are rinsed, picked and stored in sealable sandwich bags with a small wet paper towel to keep them moist.

Nutmeg Like cinnamon, nutmeg is far better when grated fresh with a microplane. I try to tell my mum this every year at Christmas over the punchbowl …

Olives We use Italian Cerignola olives in brine. They're big, fleshy and tasty. When you garnish your Martini, leave one olive in the cocktail and two in a nice shot glass on the side with a toothpick. The shot glass then becomes a holder for the pits.

Orange flower water You'll find this next to the rosewater at any good Middle Eastern food store. When adding, use a dropper or pipette to maintain control. Just a couple of drops too many and the drink will be ruined, so do be careful!

Pickled onions Buy nice big ones where possible, and store in the fridge.

Pineapple leaves Save these when juicing your pineapple. They're great for garnishes.

Rosewater We spritz this using an atomiser, which you can buy online. It spreads the aroma over the whole drink surface and looks so whimsical!

Salt flakes We use pink salt. Grind it down a little with a muddler for consistency.

Smoked paprika Keep it in a salt shaker. We buy the paprika in the cool tin with the couple on the front.

SYRUPS & MODIFIERS

Apricot syrup (3:1) Mix three parts apricot liqueur with one part sugar syrup.

Aviation N°1 (1:1:1:2) One part Monin Violet to one part Massenez Violette liqueur to one part Luxardo Maraschino liqueur to two parts sugar syrup.

This is our cheat to make the drink faster – we only have to add lemon juice and gin before shaking.

Citrus juice All citrus should be juiced fresh. A larger amount can be prepared on the day for drinks that evening, but be sure to throw it away at the end of night. Never use juice squeezed the day before. It has expired.

Coconut cream If you can't find Coco Lopez, or cream of coconut, you can make your own using store-bought coconut cream and sweetening it with cane sugar to taste.

Cream (3:1) Find the best quality cream you can. Trust me, you'll notice the difference.

Three parts quality cream to one part full-cream milk. Add to a brand new, rinsed squeeze bottle with two white sugar cubes (to help whip the cream, not to sweeten).

Shake the bottle a hundred times. (Be sure to put your finger over the nozzle first.) Shake again before each use.

Floating cream on a drink:

Shake your squeeze bottle to mix the cream. This will aerate it so it will float on the drink. Don't mix it too much, or it'll get too thick.

Aim the nozzle just above the drink and squeeze slowly. The aim is to cover the drink with a thin, even layer of cream (see *La Dominicana*, page 134).

Eggs We use fresh small organic free-range eggs.

Using egg in drinks:

Different parts of the egg are used for different styles of drinks. Do pay attention to the recipes – they might call for the white, the yolk or the whole thing.

In fancy speak …

Silver refers to a drink that has egg white only. *Golden* is when it's just the yolk. And *Royal*, well, that's just the whole damn thing.

If you learn these terms it's no drama if you accidentally drop the whole egg into a drink that calls for just the white – just tell them it's a Royal!

Fruit cup (1:1:½:¼)

For a bottle…

Mix 180 ml (6 fl oz) gin, 180 ml (6 fl oz) Cocchi sweet vermouth, 90 ml (3 fl oz) Grand Marnier and 60 ml (2 fl oz) Cherry Heering.

Or for a single serving …

Mix 30 ml (1 fl oz) gin, 30 ml (1 fl oz) Cocchi sweet vermouth, 15 ml (½ fl oz) Grand Marnier and 7.5 ml (¼ fl oz) Cherry Heering.

Ginger syrup (2:1½) Mix two parts raw ginger juice to 1½ parts caster sugar (e.g. 1 L (33½ fl oz) ginger juice to 750 g (24 oz) caster sugar).

Add sugar slowly to raw juice and stir until completely dissolved.

Grenadine (1:1) Mix equal parts pomegranate molasses to sugar syrup.

Add 2.5 ml (½ teaspoon) vanilla essence, 3.5 ml (¾ teaspoon) rosewater and 5 dashes orange bitters per litre.

Honey syrup (3:1) Mix three parts honey to one part hot water. Stir until completely mixed.

Maraschino liqueur (1:1) Mix equal parts Luxardo Maraschino liqueur and sugar syrup.

Marmalade syrup (3:1) We take the best quality marmalade and mix it down three parts to one part hot water to make it user friendly. You'll need it for your Breakfast Julep (see page 213) after a big night out.

Orange bitters (1:1) Mix equal parts Fee Brothers Orange Bitters with Regans' Orange Bitters.

Orange curaçao (1:1) Mix equal parts Grand Marnier to sugar syrup.

Orgeat (1:1) Mix equal parts orgeat syrup and sugar syrup.

Peach syrup (2:1) Mix two parts peach liqueur with one part sugar syrup.

Sugar cubes Perfect cut white and raw cubes preferred. That way you can be sure how much sugar you're getting every time.

Simple sugar syrup (1:1) Measure on scales: equal parts caster sugar and warm water.

Triple sec (3:1) Mix three parts Cointreau with one part sugar syrup.

Violet liqueur (1:1:2) One part Monin Violet syrup to one part Massenez Violet liqueur to two parts sugar syrup.

THE LIQUOR CABINET

As these are classic cocktails, you're going to come across a few liqueurs in this book that you've never heard of. Don't be alarmed, it's all quite simple. In fact, some are still lurking in your grandmother's cabinet. Seriously, I found a bottle of Cynar from the sixties in mine. Talk about striking gold!

Just remember, these are simple drinks that rely on the strengths of each component. You need a good foundation if you want to build a great drink, so don't be afraid to invest in good quality spirits.

Below are the spirits needed to make all the drinks in this book – a sort of shopping list, if you will. No chat about which monks added how many ingredients five hundred years ago …

Brandy

Apple brandy / Applejack In the US, you've got Laird's apple brandy and Applejack 'Jersey Lightning'. They're the oldest distiller of apple brandy, so I think they know what they're doing. In France, you have Calvados.

We make our own product called 'Applecrack', which we love, by blending armagnac with Pommeau de Normandie.

Cognac Must be from the Cognac region of France to be called Cognac. We use a VS (very special) Cognac for shaken drinks and VSOP (very superior old pale) for stirred and built drinks. Yes, that's what it stands for, we're not inviting you to a party …

Pisco Is it from Peru or Chile? Both countries claim the origins of this South American grape-based beauty. All I know is you can't make a Pisco Sour without it.

Fortified

Bitters We don't use too many different bitters in the bar but we treasure what we do use. It's really exciting that there are so many amazing products available now.

Angostura bitters Every house in Australia must have a bottle of this. Lemon, lime and bitters is our national drink.

Chocolate bitters Great to throw just a little curve ball in some stirred drinks with whisk(e)y or rum.

Orange bitters We blend a few different types to get the right taste for our drinks.

Peach bitters We use this one rarely. It features in the Kentucky River (aka Fox River) cocktail *(see page 189)*.

Peychaud's bitters Essential for a Sazerac cocktail *(see page 126)* and looks gorgeous in a Grapefruit Collins *(see page 67)* or Queen's Park Swizzle *(see page 110)*.

Cocchi Americano An Italian aperitif with a moscato base. It's amazing on its own and also in cocktails. Its soft, sweet, fruity quality is very versatile. Use it in shaken drinks with lemon or stir down in place of vermouth.

Cocchi Rosa I love this stuff. It's a garden party in spring surrounded by all your favourite people. A party in your mouth.

Port We use a lot of tawny Port. It's nice and rich and works a treat with our flips and fizzes. Or cheese…

Amontillado sherry Darker than fino but lighter than oloroso. Kind of like the rosé of sherry.

Cream sherry Harvey's Bristol Cream is the most popular. Artificially sweetened and made by blending mostly Pedro Ximenez and oloroso sherries. You need this for your Fog Cutter *(see page 213)*.

Manzanilla sherry Another elixir that shines only when she's fresh. We love sherry at The Everleigh. On its own, stirred down with gin or shaken into a very refreshing number.

Dry vermouth We love Dolin. It's light, delicate and delicious, and not oily or heavy. It's our favourite dry vermouth.

Bianco vermouth A step up in austerity from dry vermouth. It has the body and strength to take on some of the bigger spirits.

Sweet vermouth There is quite a lot of choice when it comes to sweet vermouth these days. They're all unique and have different offerings. We love Cocchi. I'm not a sales rep, it just floats my boat. It's light, delicate and sweet and it makes the best Manhattan *(see page 186)* and Negroni *(see pages 46 & 182)*.

Gin

All our gin cocktails are based on Plymouth and London dry-style gins. You don't want to use any vastly different flavoured gins for cocktails unless you're familiar with how they'll play out.

Liqueurs

Absinthe The real stuff. Dry and spicy and full of black licorice.

Amaretto An almond-flavoured liqueur made with apricot pits and almonds. Has a real marzipan flavour throughout.

Amaro Montenegro A very popular digestif consumed on ice with a slice of orange. It's very light and floral while still containing some great bitter herbals. Perfect for sipping after dinner.

Amer Picon A French aperitif with a strong orange flavour. Up until the last few years it was near impossible to find outside Europe. This beautiful elixir is vital in the Brooklyn cocktail *(see page 129)*.

Aperol Relatively new to the aperitif market. When I say new, she was only born in 1919. Much younger than Campari and not as strong or as bitter, which has given her a leg up in the aperitif world.

Benedictine A brandy-based liqueur that mixes perfectly with stirred or shaken cocktails. A versatile spirit, it's great on its own also.

Campari It's true, up until 2006 Campari had been using carmine dye derived from crushed cochineal insects to achieve its red colour. Love or hate the bittersweet gal, she plays an integral part in one of the most important cocktails of all time, the Negroni *(see pages 46 & 182)*.

Cherry Heering A very classic and popular brand of cherry liqueur. Always makes me think of the little fishies in a tin.

Coffee liqueur Always use a good quality coffee liqueur – we like Illy, where you get all the coffee and less of the sugar.

Cointreau A brand of triple sec from France with an intense orange flavour and a solid alcohol content to boot. We use Cointreau to blend our own triple sec, as listed in our syrups and modifiers *(see pages 33–35)*.

Drambuie A sweet, golden nectar made from Scotch whisky, honey, herbs and spices.

Fernet-Branca You love it or you hate it. It's dry and bitter but great after a meal and works wonderfully with sweet vermouth. The bartender's Jäger shot. I like it, I'm not gonna lie. I like Jäger too. There, I said it.

Galliano There's L'Autentico and there's Vanilla. Best read the label, they look very similar. This long thin bottle looks a lot like a baseball bat. I've always thought it's the first bottle I'd reach for if there were a zombie apocalypse.

Grand Marnier Cognac base with distilled essence of bitter orange and sugar. My mum loves this neat. We blend Grand Marnier with sugar syrup to make our house orange curaçao *(see page 35)*.

Green Chartreuse One word: herbaceous. It's boozy too, so if it's your first time, go easy. It's around 55% ABV – that's 110 proof. Fantastic.

Maraschino The James Brown of cherry liqueur – this guy brings the funk. Made from marasca cherries and their pits and stems, this one is unique and very special in classic cocktails. We dilute ours with sugar syrup so you get just the right amount of flavour and sweetness in every drink.

Orange curaçao See Grand Marnier, above.

Orgeat Don't like amaretto? Don't go here. This guy is marzipan central! Almonds, sugar and orange flower water. If you do like those flavours, say hello to your new friend.

Sloe gin Simply put, it's gin infused with sugar and sloe berries. If you like it in a Sloe Gin Fizz, try it with tonic. It's very refreshing.

St Germain That elderflower liqueur everyone just loves. Use it in a traditional sour with gin. That's something to write home about.

Suze French aperitif, pale yellow in colour. Its Gentian flavours allow you to use it along similar lines as Campari. Essential in the White Negroni *(see page 49)*.

Triple sec We make our own here by sweetening Cointreau. See our syrups and modifiers *(see pages 33–35)* for the recipe.

Violet liqueur We make our own *(see page 35)*. We like it. You can buy a bottle in any good liquor store.

White crème de cacao For chocolate times.

White crème de menthe We use white in our Grasshopper cocktail, and leave the colouring to the fresh mint.

Rum

Aged dark rum Don't mistake this one for any spiced rums. Find a nice aged rum that you enjoy, or ask your friendly neighbourhood bartender which rum they prefer.

Goslings Black Seal rum Can't make a Dark & Stormy *(see page 213)* without it. Get it in your bar.

Jamaican dark rum Appleton 12 Year should do the trick, unless you can find Smith & Cross, the end of the line in funky Jamaican rum as far as I'm concerned. With a bottle at 57% Navy Strength, she certainly has a kick, but what a kick it is!

Light rum I prefer a light rum from Cuba, although Flor de Caña 4 Year Extra Dry from Nicaragua makes my favourite Daiquiri to date.

Tequila

For the love of god, please don't make these drinks with a poor quality tequila! We only use quality tequila and we love the stuff. Look for 100% agave at the very least.

Mezcal Tequila's smoky little cousin. Hailing from Oaxaca, he's made slightly differently, giving a distinct flavour of smoke and earthiness.

Vodka

We don't use much vodka, but we do appreciate it. By definition vodka must be flavourless and odourless, so we find spirits like gin more interesting.

Whisk(e)y

The Americans and the Irish add the 'e' and Scots don't. Got it? Good!

American whiskey Bourbon and its spicier sister, rye whiskey. I find bourbon softer and sweeter. Don't get me wrong, bourbon can show its teeth when you get into higher proofs, but rye is normally the kid found smoking behind the school shed.

Irish whiskey They say that Guinness is a good source of iron and whiskey is the water of life. What a marketing team they have over there! Smooth and malty, Irish whiskey is a great whiskey to get to know first, as it's a little sweeter than the rest.

Scotch whisky Single malt whisky – great for stirring down in drinks. Its flavours are unique depending on the region they come from. We almost need a calendar showing off each style so we can try a new one every month.
    Blended whisky – perfect for shaken cocktails.
    Islay whisky (pronounced 'eye-la') – that's the smoky one. Also known as peaty or peated whisky.

'DRINKS UP!'

This is one of the most used phrases in The Everleigh. In fact, if you're in on the weekend you'll hear it all night long. Used by floor staff to let the bartender know a new order has been put on the bar, and by the bartender to let floor staff know drinks are ready to go, if someone shouts 'drinks up', you drop everything and get to the dispense station before the person who yelled it even closes their mouth.

As Sasha once said, 'a cocktail waits for no man' – words that we live by. Harry Craddock of the Savoy Hotel in London was once asked how quickly you should drink a cocktail. His response was 'Quickly, while it's laughing at you!' Harry was referring to the ice chips moving and disappearing on the glass as they melted and diluted the drink.

Drinks are up and it's time to get busy. Don't worry, we're right here with you. Now get a move on!

Seven steps to making a cocktail

01   Lay out your equipment ready to use. Get your booze, squeeze your citrus and prep your garnishes. Leave your glass in the freezer until you need it. Now, you remember the recipe, right?

02   Using a jigger, start building your drink.* Make sure you pour to the correct measuring line, no more no less, and make sure you're not tilting your jigger forward. Yes, it does make a difference!

03   Be sure to taste constantly as you go. When making a few different drinks at a time and holding a number of different conversations, there's a strong chance you'll slip up somewhere. Taste your Manhattan as you stir it to check its dilution and taste your Gimlet BEFORE you shake it. No point in expelling all that energy only to realise you forgot the lime …

04   Now shake. Word to the wise, you'd better have a great face when you make love because that's the face you make when you shake a cocktail. Sasha once leaned over and said that to me mid-shift. Probably for good reason...

05   Once you have finished that glorious shake, be sure to strain the drink ASAP. Don't taste it, you should have done that already. Don't look at it, don't finish up your conversation, just get it the hell out of there. It's falling apart as we speak!

06   Now that you have the strainer and glass in position, slow down. Don't strain so fast that you spill the drink outside the glass. Breathe, hold it in position, and strain slowly until all the liquid is out.

07   Now, you've just finished your perfect cocktail. Why are you staring at it? Get it to the guest ASAP so they can taste it while it's at its very best. It's dying, man!

---

*   *Handy tip: add your ingredients to the shaker in order of cheapest to most expensive. That way, if you make a mistake early on, you don't have to throw away your best booze.*

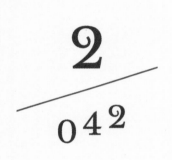

Aperitif Hour

I love a drink before dinner. In fact, one of my favourite things about eating out is sitting at the bar while I wait for a table. Forty-five minutes? No problem!

It's harder than we often realise to switch gear from work to play. Whether your work leaves you with square eyes or achy limbs, we all need a chance to defrag and refuel. The intermediary aperitif is the perfect line between your hectic day and the delicious meal to come. Whether it's a pre-game martini, something light with bubbles or a bit o' brown liquor, make sure your aperitif sets you up for the evening ahead.

NEGRONI

22 ml (¾ fl oz) **gin**
30 ml (1 fl oz) **Cocchi sweet
  vermouth**
22 ml (¾ fl oz) **Campari**
orange twist, to garnish

Build your ingredients in a
rocks glass with ice. Garnish
with an orange twist.

*Swap your gin for rye whiskey and you'll
get what acclaimed bartender Harry
MacElhone of Harry's New York Bar
in Paris called **My Old Pal**.*

'The bitters are excellent for
your liver, the gin is bad for you.
They balance each other.'
— Orson Welles, 1947

Legend has it that Count Camillo
Negroni of Florence, Italy, demanded
his favourite cocktail, the Americano,
be made with gin instead of soda.
The Negroni first made a stir around
1919 and is now internationally
recognised as the ultimate pre-dinner
cocktail.

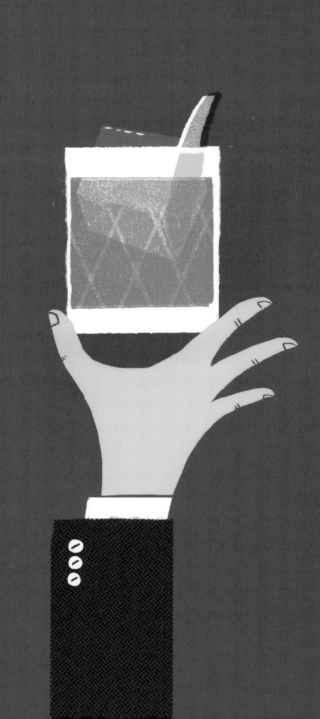

CARDINAL

45 ml (1½ fl oz) gin
22 ml (¾ fl oz) Dolin dry
vermouth
22 ml (¾ fl oz) Campari
lemon twist, to garnish

Add all your ingredients to
a mixing glass filled with ice.
Stir and strain into a frozen
cocktail glass. Garnish with
a lemon twist.

CYNARITA

45 ml (1½ fl oz) tequila
15 ml (½ fl oz) Campari
15 ml (½ fl oz) Cynar
lemon twist, to garnish

Build your ingredients in a rocks
glass with ice. Garnish with a
lemon twist.

BOULEVARDIER

Afraid you'll be judged for
drinking whiskey before dinner?
They were sipping on these
for starters way back in the
early 1920s.

45 ml (1½ fl oz) bourbon
22 ml (¾ fl oz) Cocchi sweet
vermouth
22 ml (¾ fl oz) Campari
cherry, to garnish

Add all your ingredients
to a mixing glass filled with
ice. Stir and strain into a
frozen cocktail glass.
Garnish with a cherry.

Add a dash of chocolate bitters
*to get the **Left Hand** cocktail.*

WHITE NEGRONI

45 ml (1½ fl oz) gin
22 ml (¾ fl oz) bianco
vermouth
22 ml (¾ fl oz) Suze
lemon twist, to garnish

Build your ingredients in
a rocks glass with ice.
Garnish with a lemon twist.

ARCHANGEL

This one's the result of
a collaboration between
Michael McIlroy and Richie
Boccato. Nice one, fellas.

67 ml (2¼ fl oz) gin
22 ml (¾ fl oz) Aperol
1 slice cucumber
lemon twist, to garnish

Add all your ingredients
to a mixing glass filled with
ice. Stir and strain into a frozen
cocktail glass. Garnish with
a lemon twist.

AMERICAN NEGRONI

37 ml (1¼ fl oz) bourbon
30 ml (1 fl oz) Cocchi sweet
vermouth
11 ml (⅜ fl oz) Aperol
11 ml (⅜ fl oz) Campari
1 dash Angostura bitters
lemon twist, to garnish

Build your ingredients in a rocks
glass with ice. Garnish with a
lemon twist.

NEGRONI

SIMILAR BUT DIFFERENT

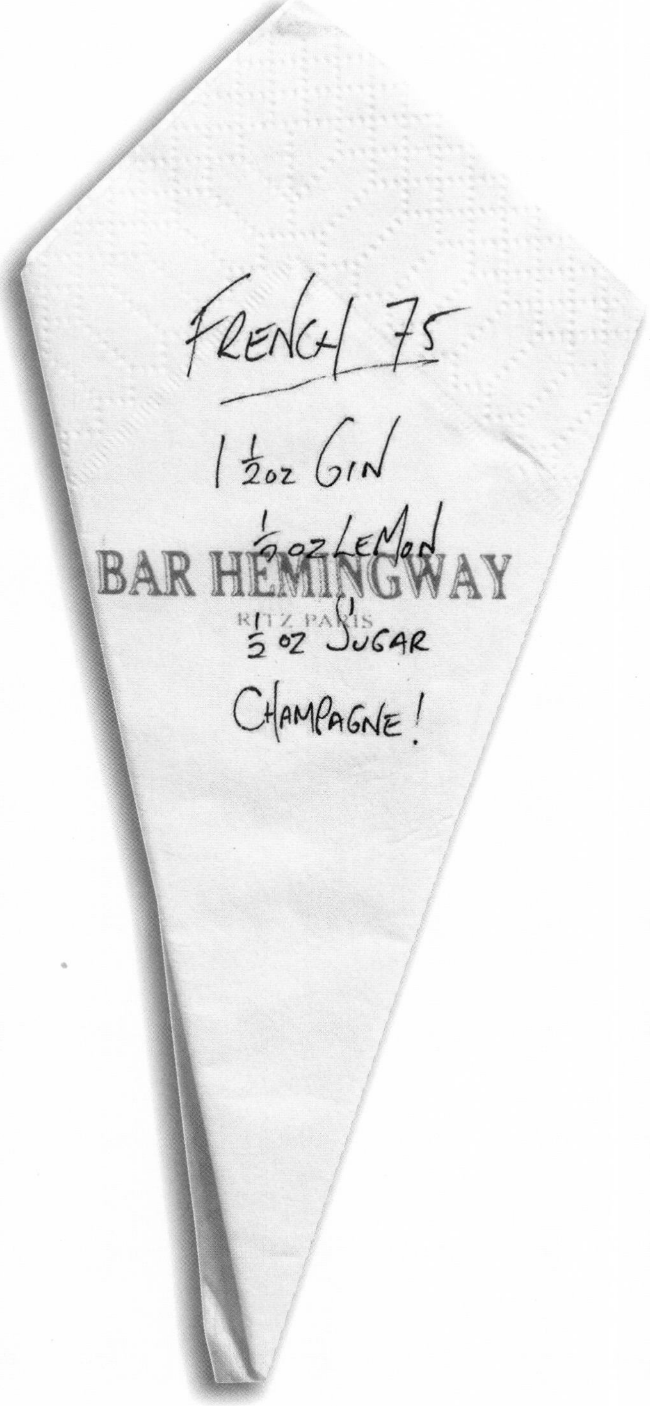

FRENCH 75

1 $\frac{1}{2}$ oz GIN

$\frac{1}{2}$ oz LEMON

$\frac{1}{2}$ oz SUGAR

CHAMPAGNE!

BAR HEMINGWAY

RITZ PARIS

FRENCH 75

30 ml (1 fl oz) **gin**
15 ml (½ fl oz) **lemon juice**
15 ml (½ fl oz) **sugar syrup**
Champagne
lemon twist, to garnish

Add all ingredients except Champagne to a shaker with ice and shake briefly. Strain into a chilled cocktail glass and top with Champagne. Garnish with a lemon twist.

Swap the sugar syrup for triple sec and you have a **Champagne Ginebra***.*

For a **French 125***, trade the gin for Cognac.*

Swap the gin for bourbon to get the **French 95***.*

Add a few dashes of absinthe and you have the **Seaplane***.*

This spirited aperitif was one of the finest drinks to come out of the Prohibition era. A derivative of the Champagne Cup (Champagne, lemon and sugar over crushed ice), the French 75 is one of a family of firecrackers.

HARRY'S PICK-ME-UP

Worked for Harry MacElhone circa 1919, works for us!

30 ml (1 fl oz) **Cognac**
15 ml (½ fl oz) **lemon juice**
15 ml (½ fl oz) **grenadine**
Champagne
lemon twist, to garnish

Add all ingredients except Champagne to a shaker with ice and shake briefly. Strain into a chilled cocktail glass and top with Champagne. Garnish with a lemon twist.

AIRMAIL

30 ml (1 fl oz) **light rum**
15 ml (½ fl oz) **lime juice**
15 ml (½ fl oz) **honey syrup**
Champagne
lime wedge, to garnish

Add all ingredients except Champagne to a shaker with ice and shake briefly. Strain into a chilled cocktail glass and top with Champagne. Garnish with a lime wedge.

LIVENER

30 ml (1 fl oz) **gin**
15 ml (½ fl oz) **lemon juice**
15 ml (½ fl oz) **sugar syrup**
2 dashes **Angostura bitters**
3 fresh **raspberries**
  (reserve 1 to garnish)
Champagne

Add all ingredients except Champagne to a shaker with ice and shake briefly. Strain into a

Switch out the Cognac for gin and you have the **Diamond Cocktail**.

This one also works beautifully with aged dark rum.

chilled cocktail glass then top with Champagne. Garnish with a fresh raspberry on a toothpick.

FORTUNE COCKTAIL

This one was inspired by a drink called the Serendipity cocktail, from the Hemingway Bar inside the Ritz Paris.

30 ml (1 fl oz) **apple brandy**
15 ml (½ fl oz) **lemon juice**
15 ml (½ fl oz) **sugar syrup**
small handful **mint leaves**
  (reserve 1 to garnish)
Champagne

Add all ingredients except Champagne to a shaker with ice and shake briefly. Strain into a chilled cocktail glass and top with Champagne. Garnish with a mint leaf.

BITTER FRENCH

One of my favourite drinks by Phil Ward, created during his days at Death & Co., NYC.

30 ml (1 fl oz) **gin**
15 ml (½ fl oz) **lemon juice**
7 ml (¼ fl oz) **Campari**
15 ml (½ fl oz) **sugar syrup**
Champagne
grapefruit twist, to garnish

Add all ingredients except Champagne to a shaker with ice and shake briefly. Strain into a chilled cocktail glass and top with Champagne. Garnish with a grapefruit twist.

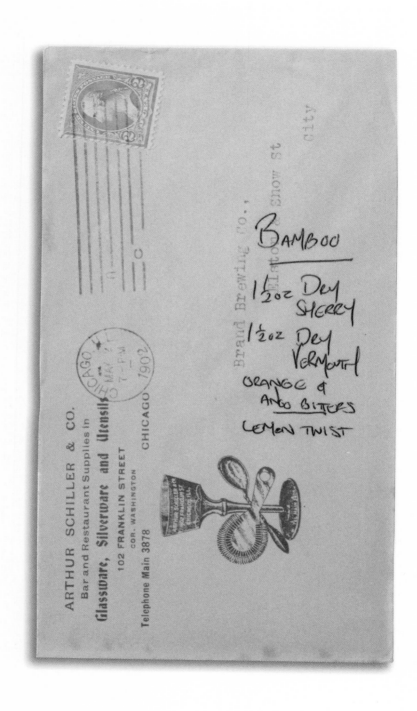

Brand Brewing Co.,
Platou & Snow St
City

BAMBOO

1½oz Dry
SHERRY

1½oz Dry
VERMOUTH

ORANGE &
ANGO BITTERS

LEMON TWIST

ARTHUR SCHILLER & CO.
Bar and Restaurant Supplies in
Glassware, Silverware and Utensils
102 FRANKLIN STREET
COR. WASHINGTON
CHICAGO
Telephone Main 3878

CHICAGO ILL
MAR 21
7 PM
1902

BAMBOO

45 ml (1½ fl oz) **fino sherry**
45 ml (1½ fl oz) **Dolin dry**
 vermouth
2 dashes orange bitters
2 dashes Angostura bitters
lemon twist, to garnish

Add all your ingredients to
a mixing glass filled with ice.
Stir and strain into a frozen
cocktail glass. Garnish with
a lemon twist.

Back in the 1890s, the Grand Hotel of Yokohama, Japan served up the Bamboo cocktail to quench the thirst of weary Western dignitaries. This elegant blend is a sophisticated choice for summer soirées. The fact that your grandma approves tells you she's one very classy lady.

ADONIS

67 ml (2¼ fl oz) fino sherry
22 ml (¾ fl oz) Cocchi sweet
  vermouth
2 dashes orange bitters
orange twist, to garnish

Add all your ingredients to
a mixing glass filled with ice.
Stir and strain into a frozen
cocktail glass. Garnish with
an orange twist.

CORONATION

60 ml (2 fl oz) manzanilla
  sherry
22 ml (¾ fl oz) Dolin dry
  vermouth
7 ml (¼ fl oz) maraschino
  liqueur
2 dashes orange bitters
lemon twist and cherry,
  to garnish

Add all your ingredients to
a mixing glass filled with ice.
Stir and strain into a frozen
cocktail glass. Garnish with
a lemon twist and a cherry.

JABBERWOCK

30 ml (1 fl oz) manzanilla
  sherry
30 ml (1 fl oz) Cocchi
  Americano
30 ml (1 fl oz) gin
2 dashes orange bitters
lemon twist, to garnish

Add all your ingredients to
a mixing glass filled with ice.
Stir and strain into a frozen

*This also works well with
light, dry sherries, such as
manzanilla or fino.*

cocktail glass. Garnish with
a lemon twist.

SHERRY COBBLER

45 ml (1½ fl oz) amontillado
  sherry
22 ml (¾ fl oz) lemon juice
22 ml (¾ fl oz) orange curaçao
seasonal berries, mint sprig
  and lemon and orange slices,
  to garnish

Build all ingredients in a frozen
double rocks glass with crushed
ice. Garnish flamboyantly with
seasonal berries, a mint sprig
and lemon and orange slices.

XERES

90 ml (3 fl oz) fino sherry
2 dashes orange bitters
2 dashes peach bitters
lemon twist, to garnish

Add all your ingredients to
a mixing glass filled with ice.
Stir and strain into a frozen
cocktail glass. Garnish with
a lemon twist.

SHERRY LADY

22 ml (¾ fl oz) manzanilla
  sherry
22 ml (¾ fl oz) gin
22 ml (¾ fl oz) lemon juice
22 ml (¾ fl oz) triple sec
lemon twist, to garnish

Add all ingredients to a shaker
with ice. Shake and strain into
a frozen cocktail glass. Garnish
with a lemon twist and discard.

BAMBOO

SIMILAR BUT DIFFERENT

AMERICANO

45 ml (1½ fl oz) **Cocchi sweet vermouth**
15 ml (½ fl oz) **Campari**
15 ml (½ fl oz) **Aperol**
30 ml (1 fl oz) **soda**
orange slice, to garnish

Build all ingredients in a frozen double rocks glass with ice. Garnish with an orange slice.

Add a little dash of absinthe to get the Young American.

'Half an hour among the jabbering loudspeakers of Ciampino Airport, time to drink two excellent Americanos, and they were on their way again ...'
    – James Bond,
    From Russia with Love

This slight variation on the classic Americano recipe includes a little Aperol, which we find brightens the drink in both appearance and flavour.

VERMOUTH PANACHE

90 ml (3 fl oz) **Dolin dry
  vermouth**
30 ml (1 fl oz) **Cocchi sweet
  vermouth**
2 dashes **Angostura bitters**
lemon twist, to garnish

Build all ingredients in a frozen
double rocks glass with ice.
Garnish with a lemon twist.

EXCELSIOR SPECIAL

When in Rome … This one
comes from the Excelsior Hotel
and has been flying well beneath
the radar for years.

45 ml (1½ fl oz) **Cocchi sweet
  vermouth**
22 ml (¾ fl oz) **Dolin dry
  vermouth**
22 ml (¾ fl oz) **Campari**
45 ml (1½ fl oz) **soda**
orange slice, to garnish

Build all ingredients in
a frozen Collins glass with ice.
Garnish with an orange slice.

BICICLETTA

75 ml (2½ fl oz) **Dolin dry
  vermouth**
45 ml (1½ fl oz) **Campari**
30 ml (1 fl oz) **soda**
orange twist, to garnish

Build all ingredients in a frozen
double rocks glass with ice.
Garnish with an orange twist.

CHAMPINO

30 ml (1 fl oz) **Campari**
30 ml (1 fl oz) **Cocchi sweet
  vermouth**
Champagne
orange twist, to garnish

Add all ingredients except
Champagne to a shaker with
ice and shake briefly. Strain into
a chilled cocktail glass and top
with Champagne. Garnish with
an orange twist.

ROME WITH A VIEW

One of my best pals in the whole
wide world, Michael McIlroy,
owns this one. Truth be told,
I really didn't like this drink
when he first came up with it,
but now I can't get enough.

30 ml (1 fl oz) **Campari**
30 ml (1 fl oz) **Dolin dry
  vermouth**
30 ml (1 fl oz) **lime juice**
22 ml (¾ fl oz) **sugar syrup**
orange slice, to garnish

Add all ingredients to a shaker
with ice and shake briefly.
Strain into a frozen Collins
glass with ice. Garnish with an
orange slice.

AMERICANO

SIMILAR BUT DIFFERENT

TOM COLLINS

60 ml (2 fl oz) **gin**
22 ml (¾ fl oz) **lemon juice**
22 ml (¾ fl oz) **sugar syrup**
soda
orange slice and cherry,
  to garnish

Add all ingredients except soda to a shaker with ice and shake briefly. Strain into a frozen Collins glass with ice and top with soda. Garnish with an orange slice and a cherry.

*Add a dash of absinthe to the Tom Collins to get the **Hayes Fizz**, named after an original Milk & Honey regular.*

Welcome to the Collins family! Tom is only the gin version, meet the rest of the clan ...

Sandy = Scotch whisky
Mike = Irish whiskey
John = genever
Pedro = rum
Jack = apple brandy
Pierre = Cognac

Each of these family members works well with fresh berries, too.

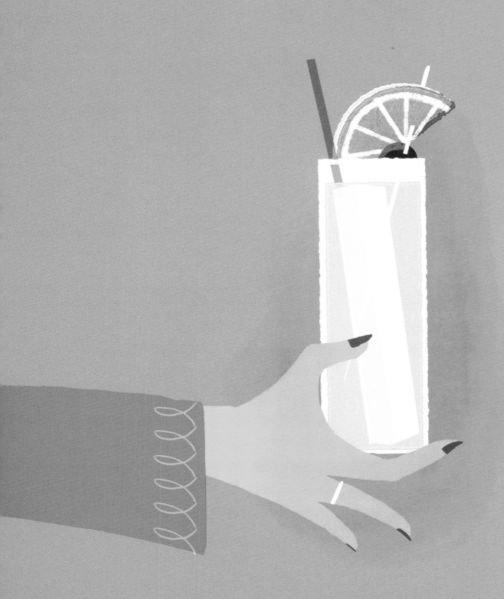

OLD CHUM'S REVIVER

60 ml (2 fl oz) **Cognac**
22 ml (¾ fl oz) **lemon juice**
22 ml (¾ fl oz) **sugar syrup**
3 **strawberries**
  (reserve 1 to garnish,
  along with a lemon wedge)
soda

Add all ingredients except
soda to a shaker and muddle.
Shake briefly and strain into
a frozen Collins glass with ice.
Top with soda and garnish with
a strawberry and a lemon wedge.

STAY UP LATE

This is a favourite from the 1946
Stork Club Bar Book. The bar
itself is steeped in history,
including the rumour that it
was where Ernest Hemingway
cashed a cheque worth the
equivalent of $1 million today.
I'm sure it was a swift walk home
that evening!

45 ml (1½ fl oz) **gin**
15 ml (½ fl oz) **Cognac**
22 ml (¾ fl oz) **lemon juice**
22 ml (¾ fl oz) **sugar syrup**
soda
lemon wedge, to garnish

Add all ingredients except
soda to a shaker with ice and
shake briefly. Strain into a
frozen Collins glass with ice
and top with soda. Garnish
with a lemon wedge.

*Cognac and strawberries are
fine friends, however this also
works well with bourbon.*

*Opt to **Stay Up Very Late** with
the addition of a cheeky dash
of absinthe!*

*Add a few dashes of Peychaud's
bitters for that little extra zing.*

*Switch grapefruit for orange
juice and you have the **Texas
Fizz**.*

JASMINE'S COOLER

Inspired by the Jasmine cocktail,
by Robert Hess.

22 ml (¾ fl oz) **gin**
22 ml (¾ fl oz) **Campari**
22 ml (¾ fl oz) **triple sec**
22 ml (¾ fl oz) **lemon juice**
soda
lemon wedge, to garnish

Add all ingredients except soda
to a shaker with ice and shake
briefly. Strain into a frozen Collins
glass with ice and top with soda.
Garnish with a lemon wedge.

GRAPEFRUIT COLLINS

An old house favourite from
the Milk & Honey days.
Adding freshly squeezed citrus
to a Tom Collins is another
great way to keep it refreshing
and exciting.

60 ml (2 fl oz) **gin**
15 ml (½ fl oz) **lemon juice**
15 ml (½ fl oz) **sugar syrup**
45 ml (1½ fl oz) **grapefruit juice**
  (or any other fresh juice)
soda
orange slice, to garnish

Add all ingredients except soda
to a shaker with ice and shake
briefly. Strain into a frozen
Collins glass with ice and top
with soda. Garnish with an
orange slice.

TOM COLLINS

SIMILAR BUT DIFFERENT

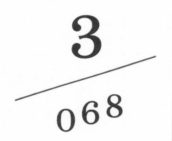

Beer

Lines on Ale

Fill with mingled cream and amber,
I will drain that glass again.
Such hilarious visions clamber
Through the chamber of my brain —
Quaintest thoughts — queerest fancies
Come to life and fade away;
What care I how time advances?
I am drinking ale today.

– Edgar Allan Poe, 1848

We've always had a soft spot for beer. A crisp pilsner on a hot day, a sour beer alongside a meal, or a stout when you don't have time for lunch – you name it, we love it. In fact, we love beer so much we made our own. And then we went a step further and opened Heartbreaker, The Everleigh's naughty little sister. She sports eight rotating taps, so we knew we'd always have somewhere to enjoy a great beer, or two …

I remember my grandfather giving me a wink as he put a splash of his beer into my lemonade. Little does he know that's how I start each shift behind the bar – just with the ratios reversed … Here are some notes on a few classic ale styles, followed by some cheeky beer and booze combos guaranteed to get you frothing.

WHAT'S YOUR STYLE?

What style of beer do you usually drink? Twenty years ago, that question was rarely heard, but today craft beer is one of the fastest emerging categories in the booze industry.

Like many other industries, the beer world has benefited from consumers' ever-increasing demand for quality, with vast numbers of craft breweries seeing great success internationally.

What does this mean for us? Well, it means we have an incredible variety of beers to choose from, all thanks to the consistent innovation and dedication of beer lovers and craft brewers alike. Hurrah!

At The Everleigh we don't pretend to be brewers or beer nerds, but we do care deeply about what goes in our pint glass. For us, beer really is the bartender's best friend. Not only do we like a shandy before a shift, we always finish with a boilermaker (a beer and a shot) – the unofficial knock-off drink for bartenders across the globe.

With this in mind, we've used the classic 'Bartender's Choice' method to help you find the beer or boilermaker for you, based on characteristics, weight and flavour. There's no right or wrong here – the one you think tastes great is the right one. And if you still don't know what you like, maybe you should just try them all!

Do you like ...

... something clean, crisp and light in flavour – a sessionable beer or summer refreshment? Try a pilsner, lager, kolsch or pale ale, followed by a bourbon chaser.

... something bigger than the lagers and pilsners, but still refreshing when served cold, particularly with a slice of lemon or orange? Opt for a wheat beer and sweeten the deal with a splash of aged dark or Jamaican rum.

... something daring and different – jam-packed full of citrus flavour and mouth-watering acidity? How about a sour beer, doubled down with a little Cognac or apple brandy.

... something a little more complex, but not too heavy? Try an amber, red, Scotch or golden ale alongside a single malt Scotch whisky.

... something big, boozy and full of hops? Jump on an IPA and wash it down with a nice and spicy rye.

... something rich and dark, malty and hoppy with roasted chocolate or toffee notes – dark in colour and low in carbonation? Make a beeline for a brown ale, porter or English bitter and fire it up with a peated Scotch whisky.

... something full and hearty with a creamy head? Go for a stout and pair it with a nice, rich amaro.

MICHELADA

1 × 355 ml (12 fl oz) **light Mexican beer**
15 ml (½ fl oz) **lime juice**
4 dashes **hot sauce**
salt flakes (for the rim)
lime wedge, to garnish

Rim a pilsner glass with salt then fill it with cracked ice. Add your hot sauce and lime and top with beer. Garnish with a lime wedge.

Maggi seasoning and Clamato juice are popular options to play with when making Micheladas.

*There's also a variation called the **Cubano** cocktail with worcestershire sauce.*

There are quite a few different ways to make your Michelada (pronounced *Mee-che-lah-dah*). You can really roll your own on this one. Personally, I love a light, preferably Mexican beer with salt, fresh lime and hot sauce.

DARK & HOPPY

A riff on the ol' family favourite, the Dark & Stormy, by our very own Zara Young.

45 ml (1½ fl oz) **Gosling's Black Seal rum**
15 ml (½ fl oz) **lime juice**
22 ml (¾ fl oz) **ginger syrup**
strong IPA
crystallised ginger, to garnish

Add all ingredients except beer to a shaker with a tiny piece of ice and whip. Pour into a frozen Collins glass with ice and top with a strong IPA. Garnish with crystallised ginger on a toothpick.

BEERHIVE

This drink featured in the 'Golden Cocktail Mile' created by The Everleigh's own Alastair Walker – twelve cocktails inspired by the twelve iconic British pubs that appeared in the 2013 film *The World's End*.

30 ml (1 fl oz) **bourbon**
22 ml (¾ fl oz) **lemon juice**
22 ml (¾ fl oz) **honey syrup**
pale ale
lemon wedge, to garnish

Add all ingredients except beer to a shaker with a tiny piece of ice and whip. Pour into a frozen Collins glass with ice and top with a crisp pale ale. Garnish with a lemon wedge.

Swap the rum for rye whiskey and you have **Dark & Hoppy #2**.

STOUT FLIP

90 ml (3 fl oz) **stout**
60 ml (2 fl oz) **Gosling's Black Seal rum**
22 ml (¾ fl oz) **sugar syrup**
1 whole egg
freshly grated nutmeg, to garnish

Give your stout a quick stir to ensure it doesn't fizz up and explode when shaking, then add all ingredients except the egg to a shaker. Add egg and dry shake to emulsify, then add ice and shake hard. Strain into a frozen cocktail glass and garnish with freshly grated nutmeg.

ANDY SHANDY

Another one from Alastair Walker, devised on a hot Melbourne summer night.

30 ml (1 fl oz) **gin**
15 ml (½ fl oz) **lemon juice**
15 ml (½ fl oz) **sugar syrup**
1 egg white
amber ale

Add all ingredients except egg white and beer to a shaker. Add the egg white and dry shake to emulsify, then add ice and shake hard. Strain into a frozen fizz glass and top with amber ale.

MICHELADA

SIMILAR BUT DIFFERENT

Wine

'Wine is one of the most civilized things in the world and one of the most natural things of the world that has been brought to the greatest perfection, and it offers a greater range for enjoyment and appreciation than, possibly, any other purely sensory thing.'

– Ernest Hemingway

I was raised under a grapevine. My grandfather's passion, aside from his family, was wine, and his backyard was covered in vines. He made his own wine with his own grapes in his own unique style. Some of my earliest memories are of the whole family separating the grapes from the stems and turning them through a home-made crusher.

While I no doubt viewed this activity as a chore at the time, I have come to relish the memories of this and similar traditions of my heritage. I even keep a photo of my grandfather's beloved garage on my wall at home, and the smell of the place is one I'll never forget.

Although cocktails are and will always be our dominant focus at The Everleigh, wine and beer also play an essential role. Like beer and its fond relationship with spirits in boilermakers and mixed drinks, wine too has a special place in the cocktail world. Without it, there'd be no vermouth, sherry or Port. Life without a Martini or a Manhattan? No thank you!

Where wine is champion, Champagne is king. The true symbol of festivity, praise and celebration, Champagne, the drink of the gods, is undeniably one of our favourite beverages and a spectacular base or addition in so many classic mixed drinks.

THE ROLE OF WINE IN COCKTAILS

From aperitifs to digestifs, wine plays an essential role in the making of cocktails. Here is a quick rundown of some of the most prevalent wine-based ingredients that appear in many of the classics.

CHAMPAGNE

Thanks to the efforts of nineteenth century Champagne houses, Champagne carries a success story like no other. First the wine of coronations, then the wine of kings, Champagne fast spread to the aristocratic elite and has been known as the symbol of both celebration and French spirit ever since.

Undeniably the best type of French toast, Champagne is used to mark some of the most memorable experiences in our lives. When it comes to cocktails there's no better way to liven things up. Whether it's with light or dark spirits, lemon or lime, berries or mint, Champagne will always make a great drink sparkle.

PORT

Only to be labelled as such if it has been made in Portugal, Port is a sweet and fruity fortified wine, popular in Australia and often taken after dinner. Here, the grape spirit is added before the fermentation process has finished, giving extra sweetness from the unfermented sugars.

Tawny and ruby are the most common styles used in cocktails. Like all wine-based products, keep it in the fridge and use within a month.

SHERRY

Sherry is a fortified wine that has been combined with a neutral grape spirit, added once the fermentation process is complete. This is then matured in a blending system called a 'solera', along with various wines of different ages.

Manzanilla, fino, amontillado, oloroso and cream sherry are the most common styles used in cocktails and they range substantially from light and crisp to rich, full and nutty.

In cocktails, lighter styles of sherry are a great alternative to dry vermouth, especially when sweeter modifiers such as maraschino liqueur and orange curaçao are also present.

Dark, rich sherries are a delicious addition to flips, ideally enjoyed after dinner.

VERMOUTH

Martini, Negroni, Manhattan – none would be the champions they are today without vermouth! Also known as aromatised wines, vermouths are fortified wines mixed with aromatic ingredients, herbs and spices.

Sadly, vermouth is one of the most mistreated products in a bar. It's astounding the number of bars that leave their opened bottles of vermouth on a shelf with a speed pourer on top. Like wine, when a vermouth is first opened it is bright and bursting with personality, but this doesn't last. Vermouth should always be stored in the fridge with a wine stopper or cork in it to slow aeration.

Sweet, dry or bianco/blanc vermouth can be enjoyed on its own, on ice or where it really makes its mark – in cocktails.

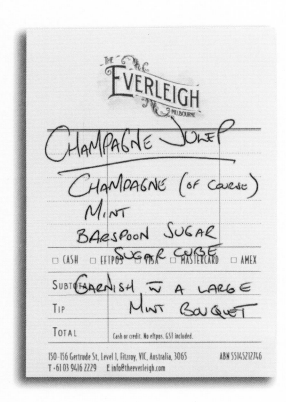

THE EVERLEIGH
MELBOURNE

CHAMPAGNE JULEP

CHAMPAGNE (OF COURSE)
MINT
BARSPOON SUGAR
SUGAR CUBE

☐ CASH   ☐ EFTPOS   ☐ VISA   ☐ MASTERCARD   ☐ AMEX

SUBTOTAL GARNISH W A LARGE
TIP   MINT BOUQUET
TOTAL   Cash or credit. No eftpos. GST included.

150-156 Gertrude St, Level 1, Fitzroy, VIC, Australia, 3065
T +61 03 9416 2229   E info@theeverleigh.com
ABN 55145212746

CHAMPAGNE JULEP

90 ml (3 fl oz) **Champagne**
1 bar spoon sugar syrup
1 white sugar cube
small handful mint leaves
mint bouquet, to garnish

Add all ingredients except Champagne to a julep cup and press with a muddler to crush the sugar cube and bruise the mint. Add Champagne and crushed ice. Swizzle briefly before topping up crushed ice. Garnish with a mint bouquet.

'I could not live without Champagne. In victory, I deserve it; in defeat, I need it!'

– Winston Churchill

The Champagne Julep is a light and fresh celebratory cocktail. It's a great example of wine acting as both the body and the personality in mixed drinks. Like any julep, that fresh mint bouquet is essential here. Bury your nose as you take your first sip for the ultimate summer refresher.

BARBOTAGE

60 ml (2 fl oz) **Champagne**
15 ml (½ fl oz) **lemon juice**
15 ml (½ fl oz) **sugar syrup**
orange twist, to garnish

Build your ingredients in a rocks
glass with ice. Garnish with an
orange twist.

CHAMPAGNE COCKTAIL

150 ml (5 fl oz) **Champagne**
1 **white sugar cube**
5 dashes **Angostura bitters**
lemon twist, to garnish

On a clean napkin, soak the
sugar cube in Angostura
bitters. Pour Champagne into
a room temperature cocktail
glass. Drop the cube into the
Champagne, being careful not
to make a splash. Garnish with
a lemon twist.

HAVE IT ALL SPRITZ

45 ml (1½ fl oz) **Champagne**
22 ml (¾ fl oz) **Aperol**
22 ml (¾ fl oz) **Cocchi
  Americano**
15 ml (½ fl oz) **Cocchi Rosa**
**orange and lemon slices,
  to garnish**

Add all ingredients except
Champagne to a wine glass with
cracked ice. Add Champagne,
then garnish with a slice each
of orange and lemon.

KITTY HIGHBALL

60 ml (2 fl oz) **dry red wine**
15 ml (½ fl oz) **lime juice**
22 ml (¾ fl oz) **ginger syrup**
soda
crystallised ginger, to garnish

Add all ingredients except soda
to a shaker and whip. Pour into
a frozen Collins glass with ice
and top with soda. Garnish
with crystallised ginger on
a toothpick.

FALLING LEAVES

This fine wine number is based
on the original, which was
created by the amazing Audrey
Saunders of Pegu Club, NYC.

45 ml (1½ fl oz) **dry riesling**
22 ml (¾ fl oz) **pear brandy or
  Poire William**
15 ml (½ fl oz) **orange curaçao**
1 dash (5 ml) **honey syrup**
3 dashes **Peychaud's bitters**
star anise, to garnish

Add your ingredients to
a mixing glass filled with ice.
Stir and strain into a frozen
cocktail glass. Garnish with
a star anise floating on top.

CHAMPAGNE JULEP

SIMILAR BUT DIFFERENT

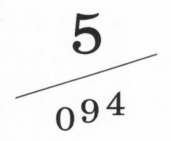

5

094

Savoury Drinks

A savoury drink isn't quite a 'liquid lunch' – it's best to think of this one as more of an entrée or a side dish. Regulars of The Everleigh know exactly how we feel about savoury drinks. Let's be honest, anything with hot sauce in it is delicious, right?

As a family we're unashamed fans of all things hot and spicy. As a result, we've taken it upon ourselves to prove there's more to savoury drinks than just the Bloody Mary. What's more, you don't have to be hungover to drink them!

What makes a savoury cocktail so exciting is the pizzazz with which weird and wonderful flavours are combined. A little muddled cucumber here, a sprinkle of black pepper there and a dash of fresh lime for good measure!

Go on, step outside that sweet, citrusy box and start with a simple salt rim. We guarantee you won't regret it.

5 LIME CHUNKS

Milk & Honey CUCUMBER SLICES

GORDON'S CUP   3/4 oz SUGAR

2oz GIN

134 Eldridge St (718) 308-6775
9 PM until 4 AM Seven Days
By appointment only Salt + Pepper

GORDON'S CUP

60 ml (2 fl oz) **gin**
5 fresh lime chunks
6 cucumber slices
  (reserve 3 to garnish)
22 ml (¾ fl oz) **sugar syrup**
salt flakes and freshly ground
  black pepper, to garnish

Add lime, cucumber and sugar syrup to a shaker and muddle. Add gin and cracked ice and shake briefly. Empty into a frozen double rocks glass. Garnish with three cucumber slices, a sprinkle of salt and black pepper.

Add a little worcestershire and hot sauce to get an even more savoury and spicy number named **Gordon's Breakfast***.*

Take a smoky chipotle hot sauce and switch gin for bourbon to get the **Square Meal** *– a drink to cover all food groups! Garnish this one with cucumber and freshly ground black pepper only.*

Like a gin Caipirinha with a little extra zing, the Gordon's Cup is another great pre-dinner option. The cucumber and fresh lime make it a crisp, light and refreshing number, while the salt and pepper adds a touch of spice and a savoury feel. The Gordon's Cup is one of Sasha's from 2005, and has been a staple among the Milk & Honey family ever since.

RED GRASSHOPPER

60 ml (2 fl oz) **tequila**
30 ml (1 fl oz) **lime juice**
22 ml (¾ fl oz) **honey syrup**
smoked paprika, to garnish

Add all ingredients to a shaker
with ice. Shake and strain into
a frozen cocktail glass.
Garnish with a light dusting
of smoked paprika.

OLD PEPPER

60 ml (2 fl oz) **bourbon**
22 ml (¾ fl oz) **lemon juice**
15 ml (½ fl oz) **sugar syrup**
2 dashes Angostura bitters
2 dashes hot sauce
2 dashes worcestershire sauce
lemon twist, to garnish

Add all ingredients to a shaker
with ice. Shake and strain into
a frozen cocktail glass. Garnish
with a lemon twist.

CHELSEA SMILE

60 ml (2 fl oz) **gin**
22 ml (¾ fl oz) **lemon juice**
22 ml (¾ fl oz) **sugar syrup**
cayenne pepper, to garnish

Add all ingredients to a shaker
with ice. Shake and strain into
a frozen cocktail glass. Garnish
with a light dusting of cayenne
pepper (go easy!).

*If you like a little smoke, swap
the hot sauce for chipotle and
only add one dash as opposed
to two.*

*Pull out the worcestershire
sauce and swap bourbon for
tequila to get the **Hot Ticket**,
another Everleigh favourite
created by our bar manager
Felix Allsop and named by
our newest recruit, Oska
Jarvis-White. Garnish that
one with some freshly ground
black pepper.*

*Substitute the gin for genever
and you have the **Holland
Razorblade**.*

OH MARY!!

One of my newest creations.
It tastes like a salad. Deeeelicious.

30 ml (1 fl oz) **gin**
22 ml (¾ fl oz) **manzanilla sherry**
15 ml (½ fl oz) **lemon juice**
15 ml (½ fl oz) **sugar syrup**
7 ml (¼ fl oz) **sherry vinegar**
2 dashes hot sauce
4 cherry tomatoes
  (reserve 1 to garnish)
freshly cracked black pepper,
  to garnish

Add all ingredients to a shaker
and muddle. Add ice and shake.
Strain into a frozen double rocks
glass with ice. Garnish with
a halved cherry tomato on a
toothpick and black pepper.

EL GUAPO

This one is by far our most
popular savoury cocktail.

60 ml (2 fl oz) **tequila**
22 ml (¾ fl oz) **sugar syrup**
5 fresh lime chunks
6 cucumber slices (reserve 3
  to garnish)
2–3 dashes Cholula hot sauce
**salt and freshly ground black
  pepper**, to garnish

Add all ingredients to a shaker
with ice. Shake and strain into
a frozen cocktail glass. Garnish
with salt and black pepper.

GORDON'S CUP

SIMILAR BUT DIFFERENT

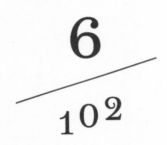

Bartender's Choice

'Bartending is an old and honorable trade. It is not a profession and I have no sympathy with those who try to make it anything but what it was. The idea of calling a bartender a professor or a mixologist is nonsense.'

– Patrick Gavin Duffy
Official Mixer's Manual, 1934

'What'll you have?'

It's fair to say that 'Bartender's Choice' is what makes the Everleigh experience so special.

When I opened the bar, I was haunted by the all-too-familiar scenario encountered when ordering a drink in a 'cocktail bar'. You know, the one where the customer is faced with a drinks menu the size of *War and Peace*, which they spend an eternity reading before eventually ordering a cocktail that they probably won't even like.

Perish the thought.

At Milk & Honey we avoided this entire awkward affair by having no menu at all, allowing every encounter with a customer to be a wholly personal and unique experience.

At The Everleigh, we believe the most important thing is getting to know our customers. To do this, we have to provide an environment where they can relax and enjoy themselves. We spend more time here than we do anywhere else, so needless to say it's a space we feel at home in. Our goal is to make everyone else feel the same way, even if it's just for one night.

All the magic here happens on the floor. The server you chat to as they top up your water will be the person telling the bartender which cocktail to make for you. The difference in The Everleigh experience is that we want to make sure you're drinking exactly what you want to drink. The success of Bartender's Choice relies on us understanding what you want out of your evening – even if you don't quite know what that is yourself! That's okay. That's the fun of it all.

So get comfy and tell us what you like, or perhaps it's easier to tell us what you don't like. Hell, tell us what you had for breakfast! Allow us to listen. Allow yourself to be surprised.

No big menu, no words you can't pronounce, no efforts to make you feel uncomfortable. Just a few questions.

So, tell me, are you after something tall, did you say?

A GUIDE TO BARTENDER'S CHOICE

Bartender's Choice involves a series of questions that engage the customer and also strengthen our relationship with them. This systematic approach allows us to navigate our way through our vast collection of classic cocktails (known as the branches) and find exactly what it is you're after.

Much like a game of 'Guess Who?', Bartender's Choice is a process of elimination that we go through together in order to find just the right drink for you.

Male, bald, beard, brown eyes, handsome? Bingo! Here's an example of how we do it with cocktails.

Spirit preference

Do you like light or dark spirits? This is almost always the first question we ask. Light spirits typically refer to gin, vodka, tequila or light rum. Dark spirits include Cognac, whisk(e)y and aged or Jamaican rum. Tequila isn't everyone's cup of tea so although we're big fans, if you don't specify that you're into it we will clarify this before moving forward.

Are there any spirits that you don't like? Most people have a gin, whisk(e)y or tequila story. Usually, it's that they stole a bottle from their parents' liquor cabinet when they were a teenager and learnt their lesson. There's only a certain extent to which we will try to broaden your horizons. If the sheer thought of a particular spirit makes you gag, we'll be sure to steer well clear.

Style of drink

Do you feel like something refreshing with citrus or something serious, stiff and boozy? Any drink shaken with ice will contain fresh citrus. However, don't confuse 'citrusy', which can simply refer to a drink containing lemon or lime, with 'fruity' or even 'sweet'. We'll get to that.

Here, we decide whether you're after something bold and booze-forward, stirred or built and served on the rocks, or something lighter, shaken with fresh citrus. There are a number of drinks that don't fit comfortably into the above two categories, but your response to this question will help us understand which end of the scale you're leaning towards.

If it's refreshing with citrus, are you after something tall with ice or short and sharp? Tall drinks, such as Collins, Rickeys, Bucks and Highballs, are topped with soda or occasionally sparkling wine. Short, sharp cocktails include sours, gimlets, daiquiris and sidecars.

Boozy and stiff more your style? You might like an Old Fashioned, Martini or Manhattan, for example. No problem. Here, we're talking either built, 'on the rocks' drinks or cocktails that have been stirred with ice. These drinks contain no fresh citrus, just straight booze and perhaps liqueurs or bitters.

If you're after something creamy and dessert-like, or a hot toddy perhaps, it's highly likely you'll tell us. If you want something short and citrusy but don't like 'fiddly cocktail glasses' we can throw a drink that's usually served 'up' in a coupette into a rocks glass with ice, no problem. It's our job to find those things out, but don't be afraid to speak up. No question is a stupid question. Well, not many are …

Flavour profile

Do you feel like something on the sweeter side, more sour and tart, or dry, spicy or bitter? Establishing what flavours you usually like, combined with what you feel like drinking right now, is really important, and the two can differ quite considerably. For example, you might generally be inclined to order a dry or even savoury-style drink, but your dinner at the restaurant around the corner was on the salty side and now you're craving something light, citrusy and slightly sweet.

The Everleigh always stocks a fresh, delicious array of seasonal fruits and flavours that changes from night to night. It's our responsibility to try each of these before a shift to see exactly where they're at before recommending them. Although we source the highest quality produce all year round, we can't deny our strawberries taste different from season to season. Therefore, the way we combine this ingredient with other citrus or modifiers to achieve a certain flavour profile may vary.

We'll take you through all the fresh ingredients we have on offer to see if any get you particularly excited. Sometimes even a subtle but curious 'oooh' is enough to put us on the right track.

Our house-made grenadine has always been a firm favourite for tart-tasting cocktails, giving citrusy drinks that perfect sweet-and-sour combo. Our ginger syrup, made from cold-pressed fresh ginger is, as you can imagine, incredibly lively and spicy! We'll always check that you love and don't simply tolerate the taste of ginger before throwing this one in the mix.

For boozy, stirred or rocks drinks without citrus, tart flavours are out the window. These drinks often deal with more complex flavours and it's important to determine whether you'd prefer something on the drier or sweeter side before moving forward. Sweetness in this case can come from anything from sweet vermouth to honey, and from chocolate bitters to Campari. Drier ingredients include dry vermouth, sherry and absinthe. In cocktails, ingredients such as absinthe and peaty whisky are used sparingly, so don't be alarmed if we make this suggestion. For example, a dash or two of absinthe can really dry out an otherwise sweeter-style drink, giving it that little extra edge and spice without overpowering the other flavours.

Drink of choice

What do you usually drink? If everyone in your group has been to The Everleigh before, we'll save you the full spiel. Not that it's long and boring, we just don't want to leave you parched for any longer than necessary. If you've had a drink in the past that you can't fully remember but would love to recreate, let us know the overarching flavours and we'll get to work.

Alternatively, if you come in every week and order a Negroni because you love our Negronis, hell, order a Negroni! It's one of the best drinks we can offer you. However, if you drink Negronis all the time and are keen to see what else is out there, why not try something similar but different? Tell us what you like about that drink and we'll do our best to find you something that follows similar rules.

Off limits

Is there anything we should avoid? Last but by no means least, it's vital that we take note of any allergies or aversions before putting pen to paper. Knowing what a customer doesn't like is just as important as knowing what they do enjoy. For this reason we'll always do a final check through the most commonly debated fruits, fixings and flavours prior to making our decision. Cream, eggs, absinthe and ginger are the big ones, but orange isn't far behind – who knew so many people didn't like orange juice?

If you are intolerant, allergic or averse to a particular product but are keen to replicate the flavour using other ingredients, do let us know. One of our most valued regulars and local business owners discovered she could enjoy a vegan Whiskey Sour with us without the egg white. For those who enjoy Amaretto sours but have to go egg-free, the Army & Navy is an equally delicious nutty mix of gin, fresh lemon and orgeat (almond liqueur) – all the flavour, none of the egg!

The proof is in the drinking

So, what do you think? The real tools of bartending are our ears, eyes and mouth. Before we begin to make drinks, it is essential we perfect the skill of communication. This is something we take very seriously. Bartender's Choice isn't as simple as answering the questions above. For example, when someone says they want a sour drink, how sour do they want it? We use our experience and training to hone a sort of inner GPS, focused on pinpointing exactly what each guest is after, and assuming it will be vastly different to what the person sitting next to them would like.

Once perfected, this method is fast, fun and exciting for all involved. Most of all, it's accurate and gives great results. Returning to a customer after they've had a sip or two to hear that it was 'exactly what I was thinking of' or to be told 'you hit the nail on the head' is why we do it. And if you don't like it, how about I have that one and we'll get you something else.

THE COCKTAIL BRANCHES

The Cocktail Branches is an enormous collection of classic and house cocktails organised in a way that's easy to navigate and quick to read. When used in conjunction with Bartender's Choice it provides enough options to keep any customer guessing all night long!

To break it down, each drink in the Cocktail Branches is placed under its 'mother' cocktail origin. Yes, 'mother'. Stay with me. Most of the drinks we make today derive from a classic cocktail composition; the drink in its simplest form. For example, sit at the bar for long enough and you'll hear something along the lines of, 'Hey Felix, what's a Waldorf again?', to which Felix will reply, 'It's a bourbon Manhattan with absinthe'. The Manhattan is the 'mother' cocktail here, and the Waldorf is a variation of this composition. Instead of a rye whiskey base, the Waldorf has bourbon. The same amount of sweet vermouth is included, but this drink features absinthe as well. The specifications remain the same as the classic Manhattan cocktail, therefore we use the Manhattan as a template.

I started compiling the Cocktail Branches back in 2006 after a conversation about not having enough drinks in the arsenal to keep a concept like Bartender's Choice from getting boring over time. I began buying all the cocktail books I could get my hands on (a habit that now borders on obsession), then proceeded to group every drink according to similarities in form, or branch, as the groups became known. Each week I took a new book and converted all the drinks. This process went on and on for years. I then shared this collection – the holy grail, as we now call it – with what was then our small family of four bars, as well as a couple of neighbouring bars run by close friends.

The Cocktail Branches now includes over 2000 cocktails listed under no more than twenty-five 'mother' categories. Although many might be regarded as similar drinks, they're all entirely unique in their own way and, in our business, that uniqueness is vital.

QUEEN'S PARK SWIZZLE

60 ml (2 fl oz) **light rum**
30 ml (1 fl oz) **lime juice**
22 ml (¾ fl oz) **sugar syrup**
1 **white sugar cube**
small handful **mint leaves**
3 dashes **Angostura bitters**
2 dashes **Peychaud's bitters**
mint sprig, to garnish

Add all ingredients except bitters to a shaker. Press with a muddler, to crush the sugar cube and bruise the mint. Pour mixture into a frozen Collins glass and top up with crushed ice. Add bitters around the inner rim of the glass and swizzle briefly. Top up with more crushed ice and garnish with a large mint sprig.

*Switch rum for gin to get the oh-so-English **Hyde Park Swizzle**.*

Known in-house as the QPS, this one's a real showstopper of a drink. Every time one goes out a wave of orders comes flooding in. Here's our house version of this Trinidadian classic by Toby Maloney of the old, old Milk & Honey crew.

HIGHLANDER HIGHBALL

60 ml (2 fl oz) Scotch whisky
15 ml (½ fl oz) lemon juice
45 ml (1½ fl oz) pineapple juice
15 ml (½ fl oz) sugar syrup
soda
2 pineapple leaves, to garnish

Add all ingredients except soda to a shaker with ice. Shake and strain into a frozen Collins glass with ice and top with soda. Garnish with pineapple leaves.

WHISKEY FREEZER

60 ml (2 fl oz) bourbon
30 ml (1 fl oz) lime juice
22 ml (¾ fl oz) sugar syrup
small handful mint
soda
mint sprig, to garnish

Add all ingredients except soda to a shaker with ice. Shake and strain into a frozen Collins glass with ice and top with soda. Garnish with a mint sprig.

FISHERMAN'S PRAYER

60 ml (2 fl oz) light rum
22 ml (¾ fl oz) lemon juice
22 ml (¾ fl oz) sugar syrup
4 fresh raspberries
  (reserve 1 to garnish)
soda

Add all ingredients except soda to a shaker with ice. Shake and strain into a frozen Collins glass with ice. Top with soda and garnish with a raspberry.

Another drink we don't make enough of, this Scotch and pineapple combo is a spectacular summer sipper.

Equally delicious with Scotch whisky if that's more your thing.

Add a dash of absinthe for the fresh and fragrant **Mint Cocktail.**

Or ditch the mint to get the **Single Standard.** *No spice, no salad. Just bourbon, lime, sugar and soda.*

If we hit land after days stranded at sea we reckon this is the first thing we'd want to sip on.

EASY STREET

This drink was thrown together by a beautiful man and inspiring bartender named Anthony Schmidt.

45 ml (1½ fl oz) gin
22 ml (¾ fl oz) lemon juice
15 ml (½ fl oz) St Germain
15 ml (½ fl oz) sugar syrup
4 slices cucumber
  (reserve 2 to garnish)
soda

Add all ingredients except soda to a shaker with ice. Shake and strain into a frozen Collins glass with ice. Top with soda and garnish with cucumber slices on the edge of the glass.

LOS ALTOS

The sweet pineapple with a little smoky mezcal is a stroke of genius – full credit to our young pup Dave Molyneaux.

45 ml (1½ fl oz) tequila
15 ml (½ fl oz) mezcal
45 ml (1½ fl oz) pineapple juice
15 ml (½ fl oz) lime juice
15 ml (½ fl oz) sugar syrup
soda
2 pineapple leaves, to garnish

Add all ingredients except soda to a shaker with ice and shake briefly. Strain into a frozen Collins glass with ice and top with soda. Garnish with two pineapple leaves.

QUEEN'S PARK SWIZZLE

SIMILAR BUT DIFFERENT

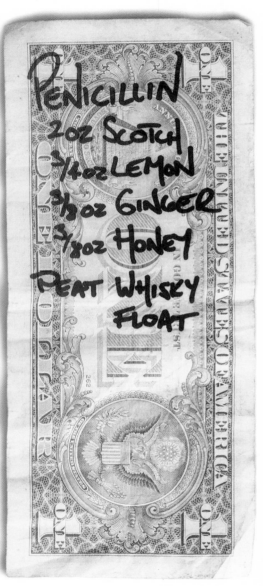

PENICILLIN

60 ml (2 fl oz) **Scotch whisky**
22 ml (¾ fl oz) **lemon juice**
11 ml (⅜ fl oz) **ginger syrup**
11 ml (⅜ fl oz) **honey syrup**
7 ml (¼ fl oz) **Islay whisky**
crystallised ginger, to garnish

Add all ingredients except the
Islay whisky to a shaker with ice.
Shake and strain into a frozen
double rocks glass with ice.
Add Islay whisky on top and
garnish with crystallised ginger
on a toothpick.

*There is a great variation of this 'modern
classic' called the* <u>*Son of a Bee Sting*</u>*, which
I personally prefer … Switch the Scotch
whisky for gin and the Islay whisky for a
spritz of rosewater. Delicious.*

Created by one of my closest and
humblest friends, Sam Ross, this is
a fiery favourite that can be found all
over the world. Slow press your ginger
to get the full effect. This medicinal
treat is guaranteed to see off a sore
throat and sniffles.

ENZONI

Created by one of the original Milk & Honey masters, Enzo Errico.

30 ml (1 fl oz) **gin**
30 ml (1 fl oz) **Campari**
22 ml (¾ fl oz) **lemon juice**
22 ml (¾ fl oz) **sugar syrup**
4 grapes (reserve 1 to garnish, along with an orange slice)

Add all ingredients to a shaker. Muddle the grapes then add ice and shake. Strain into a frozen double rocks glass with ice. Garnish with a grape and an orange slice.

GOLD RUSH

This cocktail helped many men overcome their fear of citrusy cocktails because it's served in a chunky glass over a large rock of ice. Grrr. Manly.

60 ml (2 fl oz) **bourbon**
22 ml (¾ fl oz) **lemon juice**
22 ml (¾ fl oz) **honey syrup**

Add all ingredients to a shaker with ice. Shake and strain into a frozen double rocks glass with ice.

BRAMBLE

This is my version of the late Dick Bradsell's infamous classic.

45 ml (1½ fl oz) **gin**
22 ml (¾ fl oz) **lemon juice**
22 ml (¾ fl oz) **sugar syrup**
4 blackberries
  (reserve 1 to garnish)

If you like this, try the <u>*Louisiana Purchase*</u>*, which trades bourbon for Cognac.*

The perfectly named <u>*Golden Delicious*</u> *is another great variation by NYC veteran bartender Jim Kearns – just swap the bourbon for apple brandy.*

Hello summertime! In pineapple season, everyone knows what they're drinking at The Everleigh.

You can use any berry you like with this formula, or even replace the gin with a splash of soda if you're driving.

My mate Mickey would kill me if I didn't include his variation, the <u>*Rumble*</u>*, which, as you may guess, swaps gin for light rum. Attaboy!*

Add all ingredients except gin to a shaker and muddle well. Place a third of the mixture into a frozen double rocks glass and top with crushed ice. Add the gin to the shaker then pour the rest of the mixture into the middle of the crushed ice. Top up with more ice and garnish with a blackberry.

WILD EYED ROSE

60 ml (2 fl oz) **Irish whiskey**
22 ml (¾ fl oz) **lime juice**
22 ml (¾ fl oz) **grenadine**
lime wedge, to garnish

Add all ingredients to a shaker with ice. Shake and strain into a frozen double rocks glass with ice. Garnish with a lime wedge.

PIÑA COLADA

30 ml (1 fl oz) **aged dark rum**
30 ml (1 fl oz) **Jamaican dark rum**
45 ml (1½ fl oz) **pineapple juice**
30 ml (1 fl oz) **coconut cream**
1 dash (5 ml) **lime juice**
pineapple leaf and a cherry, to garnish

Add your ingredients to a shaker. Give them a thorough stir so the coconut cream doesn't stick to the bottom. Add your ice and shake hard. Strain into a frozen double rocks glass with ice. Garnish with a pineapple leaf and a cherry.

PENICILLIN

SIMILAR BUT DIFFERENT

DAIQUIRI

As relevant now as it has ever been, this is one of the most important classic cocktails of all time.

60 ml (2 fl oz) **light rum**
30 ml (1 fl oz) **lime juice**
22 ml (¾ fl oz) **sugar syrup**
lime wedge, to garnish

Add all ingredients to a shaker with ice. Shake and strain into a frozen cocktail glass. Garnish with a lime wedge.

DOVETAIL

45 ml (1½ fl oz) **tequila**
15 ml (½ fl oz) **maraschino liqueur**
30 ml (1 fl oz) **grapefruit juice**
15 ml (½ fl oz) **lime juice**
2 dashes Peychaud's bitters
lime wedge, to garnish

Add all ingredients to a shaker with ice. Shake and strain into a frozen cocktail glass. Garnish with a lime wedge.

GIMLET

60 ml (2 fl oz) **gin**
30 ml (1 fl oz) **lime juice**
22 ml (¾ fl oz) **sugar syrup**
lime wedge, to garnish

Add all ingredients to a shaker with ice. Shake and strain into a frozen cocktail glass. Garnish with a lime wedge.

*Feeling fresh? Add a little mint to the classic Daiquiri and you have the **Maison Charles**.*

*Like mint but prefer aged rum to light? The **Brugal Cocktail** is an aged rum Daiquiri with fresh mint. Just what the doctor ordered.*

*Feeling fruity? The **Cuban Cocktail #3** is another light rum number that makes great use of apricot liqueur in place of sugar syrup. Pull back your lime to 22 ml (¾ fl oz) for this one.*

*Stick with light rum and swap your sugar for honey to get a long-time customer favourite, the **Honeysuckle**. The same drink with Jamaican rum and a splash of Angostura bitters is known as the **Brooklynite**. This drink also works beautifully with tequila – that one's known as the **Juschu**.*

*Fancy something tangy with aged rum? Swap the sugar syrup for grenadine and add mint to get another big seller, the **Detroit Daisy**.*

Or for a quick fruity fix, simply add fresh berries to the classic daiquiri.

*A great variation on the popular **Hemingway Daiquiri**, which became a sugar-free favourite of Ernest's after his diabetes diagnosis. Our own master bartender and ice wizard, Andy Chu, dropped this little grenade on us in 2015 and it made it onto the Everleigh menu within the week.*

Another back to basics champion. This classic cocktail is singlehandedly responsible for some of the most popular drinks all over the world today.

*First up are the freshest. A Gimlet with mint is called the **Southside**, and the same drink with a slice of cucumber in the shaker is called the **Eastside**. Fancy it on ice? Simply throw the Eastside on the rocks to get the **Old Maid**.*

*As with so many of our drinks, you can opt to have yours served tall or short. A Gimlet served in a tall glass becomes a **Rickey**. The same formula applies – gin, lime and sugar – tall drinks are simply topped up with a splash of soda. The **Southside Rickey** is a great example. Love a Southside but want something tall with ice? You know what to do!*

*Named after an old Milk & Honey regular, Michael Tritter, the **Tritter Rickey** is simply a Southside Rickey with a little absinthe. And what a welcome addition it is!*

*Getting back to basics now, a Gimlet with a little Angostura is known as the **Bennett**. Vary the Bennett by using apricot liqueur in place of sugar syrup and you have the **Barnum was Right**. There's a largely debated story behind this name, thanks to PT Barnum, but we wouldn't want to get sidetracked …*

*A Gimlet with honey syrup in place of sugar is called the **Business** (pronounced Beeza-neiss). Nice one, Sasha. This liquid gold also works nicely with the addition of egg white.*

*Our go-to for those who are after a Cosmo, the **Debutante** is a Gimlet that trades sugar for grenadine with a little less lime (22 ml/¾ fl oz) and a dash of orange bitters. Add a little absinthe to this one and you have another Everleigh favourite, the **Professor**.*

Last but not least, the Gimlet works beautifully with fresh berries. Try strawberry, raspberry or blueberry for a pop of colour and big burst of flavour.

GIN SOUR

... or 'non-traditional sour', as we would call it in the Cocktail Branches to clearly distinguish it from the traditional gin sour, which includes egg white.

60 ml (2 fl oz) **gin**
22 ml (¾ fl oz) **lemon juice**
22 ml (¾ fl oz) **sugar syrup**

Add all ingredients to a shaker with ice. Shake and strain into a frozen cocktail glass.

SIDECAR

45 ml (1½ fl oz) **Cognac**
22 ml (¾ fl oz) **lemon juice**
22 ml (¾ fl oz) **triple sec**
lemon twist, to garnish

Add all ingredients to a shaker with ice. Shake and strain into a frozen cocktail glass. Garnish with a lemon twist.

WHISKEY SOUR

60 ml (2 fl oz) **bourbon**
22 ml (¾ fl oz) **lemon juice**
22 ml (¾ fl oz) **sugar syrup**
1 egg white
Angostura bitters, to garnish

Add all ingredients to a shaker and dry shake to emulsify. Add ice and shake hard, then strain into a frozen sour glass. Garnish with an Angostura stripe.

Add a dash of Angostura bitters for the __Fitzgerald__, named by King Cocktail himself, the man with all the charm, Mr Dale Degroff.

Make it traditional by adding an egg white and you've got David Embury's classic __Montreal Sour__, featured in the 1948 text The Fine Art of Mixing Drinks.

For something a touch more refreshing, add mint to the Gin Sour to get the __Iris Cocktail__.

Swap the sugar syrup for peach liqueur and you have the __Serpent's Tooth__. Add egg white to this one and you'll get the __Perfect Lady__, a great drink that was discovered in a cocktail competition in 1936.

Swap that sugar syrup out once more, this time for honey syrup, and you have another golden oldie that came out of The Ritz, Paris in 1936, perfectly dubbed the __Bee's Knees__. Add a couple of muddled strawberries to this guy and you've got yourself a real party.

The __Aviation__, another well-known classic, similarly derives from the Gin Sour formula. __Aviation #1__ is the violet version from Hugo Ensslin's 1916 book Drinks as They are Mixed. *To fix up this floral number, swap the sugar syrup for Aviation No. 1 mix (see page 33) and garnish with a cherry or two.*

For the __Aviation #2__, found in the Savoy Cocktail Book, published in 1930, simply swap the sugar syrup for maraschino liqueur.

After something similar but different? Add orange bitters to the Aviation #2 to get the __Casino__, or use Angostura bitters to get the __Betty James__.

The __Chevalier__ is one of the Sidecar's lesser-known siblings. This one calls for a dash of Angostura bitters for a little more conversation.

For a little extra kick, trade Cognac for Scotch whisky and you have the __Prosperity__ cocktail.

Go bare if you dare – the __Commando__ is a delicious bourbon Sidecar with a cheeky dash of absinthe.

The __Chelsea Sidecar__ is of course the gin version. Add Angostura bitters to this one and you have the __Fine & Dandy__. Hold the bitters and add egg white to the Chelsea Sidecar for that well-known classic, the __White Lady__. Hold the egg but add a dash of absinthe to the Chelsea Sidecar to get the __Queen Elizabeth__ when served up, or the __Hocus Pocus__ if it's on crushed ice.

Can't decide between the gin and Cognac versions? Opt for the outspoken spawn of the classic Sidecar and the Chelsea Sidecar, better known as the __Loud Speaker__. This one is made with equal parts gin and Cognac.

Trade the bourbon for Cognac and you have the __Brunswick Sour__.

Prefer pisco? Do a straight swap for another favourite, __Pisco Sour__. Garnish this one with freshly grated cinnamon and an Angostura stripe.

Swap the bourbon for rye whiskey and you have the __Continental Sour__. Add a dash of absinthe to this one for the nicely spicy __Rattlesnake Cocktail__.

Can't decide between a glass of red and a cocktail? Try a traditional bourbon sour on the rocks with a splash of red wine to get the deep and delicious __New York Sour__.

AUTHORIZED

FRIGIDAIRE AND McCRAY
DEALER

PHONE: JE. 8-4250

FISHER & HUGHES, INC.

SODA MASTER - ICE CUBERS

REFRIGERATION AND AIR CONDITIONING

RESTAURANT AND STORE FIXTURES

SALES AND SERVICE

LEO G. BLACK

79 WASHINGTON STREET
MORRISTOWN, N.J.

Bobby Burns No. 2   1½ oz Scotch
½ oz Sweet Vermouth
¼ oz Maraschino

Lemon Twist

BOBBY BURNS #2

45 ml (1½ fl oz) **Scotch whisky**
15 ml (½ fl oz) **Cocchi sweet
vermouth**
7 ml (¼ fl oz) **maraschino
liqueur**
lemon twist, to garnish

Build in a rocks glass with ice.
Garnish with a lemon twist.

*Switch maraschino liqueur for Benedictine
to get the **Bobby Burns #1**, or use
Drambuie for the **Bobby Burns #3**.*

I know I've started something with number 2, but sometimes the sequel really is better than the original. At least, we think so …

I stumbled upon this one later on in the game in a book given to me by Greg Boehm of Cocktail Kingdom, called *1700 Cocktails for the Man Behind the Bar* by R. de Fleury, 1934.

FANCY FREE

60 ml (2 fl oz) **bourbon**
15 ml (½ fl oz) **maraschino liqueur**
1 dash orange bitters
2 dashes Angostura bitters
orange twist, to garnish

Build in a rocks glass with ice. Garnish with an orange twist.

COASTER

This guy is simply a classic Pink Gin served on the rocks. One for those whose gin face is well and truly behind them …

60 ml (2 fl oz) **gin**
5 dashes Angostura bitters
lemon twist, to garnish

Build in a rocks glass with ice. Garnish with a lemon twist.

TATTLETALE

Disappointed to hear of people being unable to make his Penicillin for lack of citrus and ginger, Sam Ross put this little boozy version together.

45 ml (1½ fl oz) **Scotch whisky**
15 ml (½ fl oz) **Islay whisky**
1 bar spoon honey syrup
3 dashes Angostura bitters
lemon twist, to garnish

Build in a rocks glass with ice. Garnish with a lemon twist.

CHET BAKER

Another one from Sam Ross. This one's a dedication to the great jazz legend we all enjoyed listening to on repeat at Milk & Honey …

60 ml (2 fl oz) **aged dark rum**
2 bar spoons Cocchi sweet vermouth
1 bar spoon honey syrup
3 dashes Angostura bitters
orange twist, to garnish

Build in a rocks glass with ice. Garnish with an orange twist.

MONTE CARLOS

This one's from Chris Bostick, a man with a great smile out of Austin, Texas with a fine bar called Half Step – a must visit on Rainey Street.

60 ml (2 fl oz) **Reposado tequila**
15 ml (½ fl oz) **Benedictine**
2 dashes Angostura bitters
lemon twist, to garnish

Build in a rocks glass with ice. Garnish with a lemon twist.

THE HIGHLANDER

Our brother from another mother, Eric Alperin of the Varnish, Los Angeles, gets a high five for this tasty number.

60 ml (2 fl oz) **Scotch whisky**
15 ml (½ fl oz) **Cherry Heering**
lemon twist, to garnish

Build in a rocks glass with ice. Garnish with a lemon twist.

BOBBY BURNS #2

SIMILAR BUT DIFFERENT

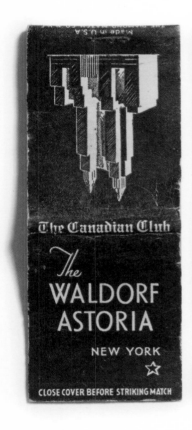
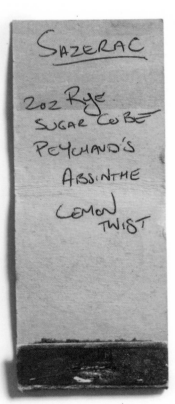

SAZERAC

60 ml (2 fl oz) **rye whiskey**
1 white sugar cube
3 dashes Peychaud's bitters
absinthe, to rinse
lemon twist, to garnish

Add the sugar cube and bitters to a mixing glass. Crush the cube with a muddler and add rye. Add ice and stir. Fill a Sazerac glass with crushed ice to chill. Empty the ice then rinse with the absinthe and drain (or drink). Strain the drink into the glass and garnish with a lemon twist.

The lemon twist is essential, but as Stanley Clisby Arthur declared in his 1937 text Famous New Orleans Drinks and How to Mix 'em, *'do not commit the sacrilege of dropping the peel into the drink'. Squeeze the twist over the top of the drink to expel the oils then lay it across the top of the glass.*

This was the very first drink I had at Little Branch back in 2005. There are four drinks that made me fall so deeply in love with cocktails – the Sazerac, the Gin Gin Mule, the New York Flip and the Montreal Sour. This drink really is a masterpiece. The original called for Cognac instead of rye, and the brand of Cognac used was called Sazerac – hence the name. Today, the most popular version calls for rye whiskey. If a mixture of rye and Cognac is used, we call it a New York Sazerac.

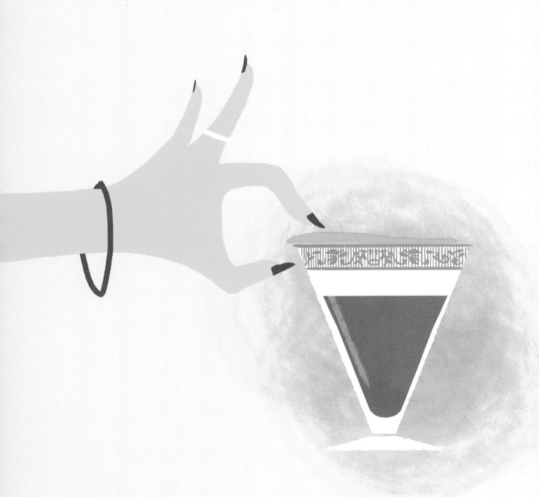

BERLIONI

If you haven't yet had the pleasure, meet Cynar, our artichoke-flavoured friend. Be cool. He's one of us.

45 ml (1½ fl oz) **gin**
22 ml (¾ fl oz) **Cynar**
15 ml (½ fl oz) **Dolin dry vermouth**
orange twist, to garnish

Add your ingredients to a mixing glass with ice. Stir and strain into a frozen cocktail glass. Garnish with an orange twist.

BROOKLYN

A dry Manhattan variation to die for – there was no way I could have left this drink out of this book. The zesty addition of Amer Picon is a game changer, and it's a game we never tire of.

60 ml (2 fl oz) **rye whiskey**
15 ml (½ fl oz) **Dolin dry vermouth**
7 ml (¼ fl oz) **maraschino liqueur**
7 ml (¼ fl oz) **Amer Picon**
cherry, to garnish

Add your ingredients to a mixing glass with ice. Stir and strain into a frozen cocktail glass. Garnish with a cherry.

Throw this one on the rocks to get a __Flushing__ cocktail.

After something spicy? Go for the __Bughouse__ – a Harvard with a dash of absinthe.

Credit once again goes to Mr Allsop for this smooth sipper. Oh Felix, Jamaican-us crazy!

Our neighbourhood namesake, the __Fitzroy__ cocktail, is one of our all-time favourite smoky sippers. Here we have to cut the Scotch whisky down to 45 ml (1½ fl oz) and add in 15 ml (½ fl oz) Islay whisky.

For a 'perfect' Rob Roy (a 'perfect' cocktail refers to a version of a drink with an even split of sweet and dry vermouths), otherwise known as the __Affinity__ cocktail, go half sweet and half dry vermouth (15 ml/½ fl oz of each). Garnish this with a lemon twist. This drink on the rocks is known as the __Beals__ cocktail.

How about a holiday? Add a Drambuie rinse to the Affinity cocktail and you have seventies throwback, the __Holiday Style Rob Roy__.

HARVARD

60 ml (2 fl oz) **Cognac**
30 ml (1 fl oz) **Cocchi sweet vermouth**
3 dashes **Angostura bitters**
cherry, to garnish

Add your ingredients to a mixing glass with ice. Stir and strain into a frozen cocktail glass. Garnish with a cherry.

KINGSTON

60 ml (2 fl oz) **12yr Jamaican rum**
15 ml (½ fl oz) **Dolin dry vermouth**
7 ml (¼ fl oz) **amaro Montenegro**
1 bar spoon **orange curaçao**
orange twist, to garnish

Add your ingredients to a mixing glass with ice. Stir and strain into a frozen cocktail glass. Garnish with an orange twist.

ROB ROY

60 ml (2 fl oz) **Scotch whisky**
30 ml (1 fl oz) **Cocchi sweet vermouth**
3 dashes **Angostura bitters**
cherry, to garnish

Add your ingredients to a mixing glass with ice. Stir and strain into a frozen cocktail glass. Garnish with a cherry.

Digestifs

Nothing completes a great dining experience like a timely digestif. A simple toast, such as an amaro or fortified, is a fitting way to finish the meal, but if you really want to celebrate your empty plate, opt for a cocktail. Never is a customer more sure of what they want to drink than after a big meal …

'I stupidly skipped dessert and need a sweet and creamy fix!'

'I'm so full and sleepy, maybe something citrusy and light to pick me up?'

'I do love Port … can you do a cocktail with that?'

'We've been drinking wine all night. I'm ready for some real liquor.'

Hold on, we've got just the thing …

sasha.petraske@gmail.com   (212) WAtkins 9-9597

LA DOMINICANA
1½ oz AGED RUM

Sasha Petraske

1½ oz COFFEE LIQ
TOP w̄ HAND WHIPPED
                    CREAM

26 Jones Street, New York 14, New York

LA DOMINICANA

45 ml (1½ fl oz) **aged dark rum**
45 ml (1½ fl oz) **coffee liqueur**
hand-whipped cream

Add all ingredients except cream to a mixing glass with ice. Stir, then strain into a frozen cocktail glass. Float a thin layer of hand-whipped cream on top.

Feel free to swap the base for tequila, Scotch whisky or American whiskey if you fancy. Each is as delicious as the next!

The vodka substitute is our house version of the **White Russian**.

Aged rum and coffee are fine friends. The simple addition of a thin float of good quality hand-whipped cream on the top of this drink gives a smooth, rounded mouthfeel. La Dominicana is a Milk & Honey original from 2001. Everleigh customers can't get enough.

GOLDEN CADILLAC

This drink, also known as
'Creamy Town' to some
of our doting regulars, is
the most unapologetic of
dessert cocktails.

45 ml (1½ fl oz) **white crème
de cacao**
45 ml (1½ fl oz) **orange juice**
30 ml (1 fl oz) **cream**
15 ml (½ fl oz) **Galliano vanilla
orange slice, to garnish**

Add all ingredients to
a shaker with ice. Shake and
strain into a frozen double
rocks glass with ice. Garnish
with a slice of orange.

BEE'S KISS

Far better than being kissed by
a bee in our opinion! Simplicity
trumps again. Dessert drinks
don't get better than this.

60 ml (2 fl oz) **aged dark rum**
22 ml (¾ fl oz) **honey syrup**
22 ml (¾ fl oz) **cream**

Add all ingredients to a shaker
with ice. Shake and strain into a
frozen cocktail glass.

GRASSHOPPER

This one's our house version
of the classic mint choc-cream
wonder. The least guilty
of pleasures.

37 ml (1¼ fl oz) **white crème
de menthe**
37 ml (1¼ fl oz) **white crème
de cacao**

*Not a fan of Cognac? Try this
one with gin – it's equally
delicious!*

30 ml (1 fl oz) **cream
small handful fresh mint
leaves (reserve 1 to garnish)**

Add all ingredients to
a shaker with ice. Shake and
strain into a frozen cocktail
glass. Garnish with a mint leaf.

CAFFÉ CON LECHE

The great Melbourne native
Sam Ross is the proud father
of this delicious drink.

30 ml (1 fl oz) **Gosling's Black
Seal rum**
22 ml (¾ fl oz) **coffee liqueur**
22 ml (¾ fl oz) **sugar syrup**
15 ml (½ fl oz) **cream**
**1 egg yolk
freshly grated nutmeg,
to garnish**

Add all ingredients except egg
yolk to a shaker. Add the egg
yolk and dry shake to emulsify.
Add ice and shake hard.
Strain into a frozen cocktail
glass and garnish with freshly
grated nutmeg.

BRANDY ALEXANDER

45 ml (1½ fl oz) **Cognac**
30 ml (1 fl oz) **white crème
de cacao**
30 ml (1 fl oz) **cream
freshly grated nutmeg,
to garnish**

Add all ingredients to a shaker
with ice. Shake and strain into
a frozen cocktail glass. Garnish
with freshly grated nutmeg.

LA DOMINICANA

SIMILAR BUT DIFFERENT

LE COQ ROUGE, COCKTAIL LOUNGE

LE COQ ROUGE
65 EAST 56th STREET
NEW YORK CITY
PLaza 3-8887
Cocktails, Dinner, Dancing

Gin Fizz
2oz Gin
3/4 oz Lemon
3/4oz Sugar
Egg White
Soda

6-

POST CARD

EAST & WEST PUB. CO., INC., 140 W. 42ND ST., N.Y.C. MADE IN U.S.A.

You
address
we stamp
and mail

GIN FIZZ

60 ml (2 fl oz) **gin**
22 ml (¾ fl oz) **lemon juice**
22 ml (¾ fl oz) **sugar syrup**
1 egg white
soda
lemon wedge, to garnish

Add all ingredients except egg white and soda to a shaker. Add the egg white and dry shake to emulsify. Add ice and shake hard. Strain into a short frozen fizz glass and top with soda. Garnish with a lemon wedge.

Swap the soda for a little Champagne and you have the __Diamond Fizz__.

Keep the soda and add some fresh mint to get the __Bootleg Fizz__.

Still hungry after dinner? Save your yolk in a small shot glass or egg cup and season it with a little salt, pepper, hot sauce and worcestershire sauce. Knock back the yolk before digging in to your gin fizz. This hearty combo is known as the __Electric Current Fizz__.

Cut your gin back to a 45 ml (1½ fl oz) measure and add 15 ml (½ fl oz) violet liqueur to get floral favourite, the __Violet Fizz__.

A fizz is a unique drink style. Like the traditional gin sour, this one is shaken with egg white and served without ice, however the fizz is presented in a short, thin tumbler, charged with a dash of soda. This one is not designed to be sipped – knock it back while it's alive and kicking. Like the Collins family, the fizz works with different base spirits and welcomes the addition of berries, fresh mint or liqueurs.

GIN GIN MULE

This one's a house version of a modern classic by Audrey Saunders of the Pegu Club, NYC.

60 ml (2 fl oz) gin
30 ml (1 fl oz) lime juice
15 ml (½ fl oz) ginger syrup
15 ml (½ fl oz) sugar syrup
small handful mint leaves
   (reserve 1 to garnish)
soda
crystallised ginger, to garnish

Add all ingredients except soda to a shaker with ice and shake briefly. Strain into a frozen Collins glass with ice and top with soda. Garnish with a mint sprig and some crystallised ginger on a toothpick.

CHAMPS ÉLYSÉES

Refreshing, vegetal and complex all at once.

45 ml (1½ fl oz) Cognac
15 ml (½ fl oz) green
   Chartreuse
22 ml (¾ fl oz) lemon juice
15 ml (½ fl oz) sugar syrup
2 dashes Angostura bitters
lemon twist, to garnish

Add all ingredients to a shaker with ice. Shake and strain into a frozen cocktail glass. Garnish with a lemon twist.

ORGEAT PUNCH

60 ml (2 fl oz) Cognac
22 ml (¾ fl oz) lemon juice

Swap the gin for Cognac to get the Sleepyhead Cocktail.

22 ml (¾ fl oz) orgeat
1 dash tawny Port
mint sprig and a cherry,
   to garnish

Build all ingredients except Port in a frozen double rocks glass with crushed ice. Mix briefly then top with more crushed ice. Add a dash of Port on top and garnish with a mint sprig and a cherry.

INFANTE

This one was put together by an old friend, Giuseppe Gonzalez.

60 ml (2 fl oz) tequila
30 ml (1 fl oz) lime juice
22 ml (¾ fl oz) orgeat
freshly grated nutmeg,
   to garnish

Add all ingredients to a shaker with ice. Shake and strain into a frozen double rocks glass with ice. Garnish with freshly grated nutmeg.

20TH CENTURY

45 ml (1½ fl oz) gin
22 ml (¾ fl oz) lemon juice
22 ml (¾ fl oz) white crème
   de cacao
22 ml (¾ fl oz) Cocchi
   Americano
lemon twist, to garnish

Add all ingredients to a shaker with ice. Shake and strain into a frozen cocktail glass, then garnish with a lemon twist.

GIN FIZZ

SIMILAR BUT DIFFERENT

APOTHEKE

30 ml (1 fl oz) **Fernet-Branca**
30 ml (1 fl oz) **white crème
   de menthe**
30 ml (1 fl oz) **Cocchi sweet
   vermouth**
cherry, to garnish

Add all ingredients to a mixing
glass with ice. Stir and strain
into a frozen cocktail glass.
Garnish with a cherry.

This little star was flying over bars in Paris in the 1920s following its publication in *Harry's ABC of Mixing Cocktails*, by Harry MacElhone in 1919. I love this drink. It is unapologetically rich and intense; the mint and Fernet-Branca make a perfect after-dinner pair.

PORTO FLIP

60 ml (2 fl oz) tawny Port
7 ml (¼ fl oz) Benedictine
7 ml (¼ fl oz) sugar syrup
1 egg yolk
freshly grated nutmeg,
    to garnish

Add all ingredients except egg yolk to a shaker. Add the egg yolk and dry shake to emulsify. Add ice and shake hard. Strain into a frozen cocktail glass and garnish with freshly grated nutmeg.

WHOLE LOTTA ROSA

There's a nice juxtaposition between this pink drink and the AC/DC song it was named after.

45 ml (1½ fl oz) Cocchi Rosa
15 ml (½ fl oz) gin
22 ml (¾ fl oz) lemon juice
15 ml (½ fl oz) sugar syrup
3 orange slices
    (reserve 1 to garnish)
1 egg white
soda

Add all ingredients except egg white and soda to a shaker. Add the egg white and dry shake to emulsify. Add ice and shake hard. Strain into a frozen fizz glass and top with soda. Garnish with an orange slice.

PRECURSORY COCKTAIL

This is a wonderful original from Tim Phillips, co-owner of Bulletin Place in Sydney.

45 ml (1½ fl oz) tawny Port
45 ml (1½ fl oz) Carpano
    Antica sweet vermouth
7 ml (¼ fl oz) lemon juice
15 ml (½ fl oz) sugar syrup
2 dashes Angostura bitters
2 dashes orange bitters
lemon twist, to finish

Add all ingredients to a mixing glass with ice. Stir and strain into a frozen cocktail glass. Garnish with a lemon twist.

L'APPETIT

45 ml (1½ fl oz) Cocchi sweet
    vermouth
30 ml (1 fl oz) Fernet-Branca
orange twist, to garnish

Build all ingredients in a rocks glass with ice. Garnish with an orange twist.

KLONDYKE

30 ml (1 fl oz) Dolin dry
    vermouth
30 ml (1 fl oz) Cocchi sweet
    vermouth
15 ml (½ fl oz) lemon juice
22 ml (¾ fl oz) ginger syrup
soda
crystallised ginger, to garnish

Add all ingredients except soda to a shaker with a tiny piece of ice and whip. Pour into a frozen Collins glass with ice and top with soda. Garnish with crystallised ginger on a toothpick.

STINGER

60 ml (2 fl oz) **Cognac**
22 ml (¾ fl oz) **white crème**
  de menthe
mint bouquet, to garnish

Build all ingredients in a frozen double rocks glass with crushed ice. Give a little swizzle and top up the crushed ice. Garnish with a mint bouquet.

Switch Cognac for Port and you have the **Port Stinger**.

With the simple but spicy addition of a sprinkling of cayenne pepper on top, the classic Stinger becomes the **Devil Cocktail**.

Add a dash of absinthe to get the **Midnight Stinger**.

Throw that Midnight Stinger on the rocks and you have the **Stinger Royal**.

'Stingers, and keep them coming.'
– Cary Grant, in 1957 movie
Kiss Them For Me

A pre-prohibition drink indeed. Story goes this one was a firm favourite among the flyboys of World War II and aristocracy of the time. At The Everleigh we serve ours on crushed ice, garnished with a big bouquet of fresh mint.

DROWSY GIRL

Terrible name, great drink. We dug this one out of Charles Baker's 1951 *South American Companion*. A delicious riff on that well-known creamy classic, the Brandy Alexander.

60 ml (2 fl oz) **Cognac**
15 ml (½ fl oz) **white crème de cacao**
7 ml (¼ fl oz) **orgeat**
cherry, to garnish

Build ingredients in a rocks glass over ice. Stir briefly, then garnish with a cherry.

TORONTO

60 ml (2 fl oz) **rye whiskey**
22 ml (¾ fl oz) **Fernet-Branca**
7 ml (¼ fl oz) **sugar syrup**
orange twist, to garnish

Add all ingredients to a mixing glass with ice. Stir and strain into a frozen cocktail glass. Garnish with an orange twist.

HANKY PANKY

This drink was created by Ada Coleman of the Savoy Hotel, London, in the 1920s and remains a favourite of bartenders worldwide. Only one way to find out why …

60 ml (2 fl oz) **gin**
22 ml (¾ fl oz) **Cocchi sweet vermouth**
7 ml (¼ fl oz) **Fernet-Branca**
orange twist, to garnish

Add all ingredients to a mixing glass with ice. Stir and strain into a frozen cocktail glass. Garnish with an orange twist.

LITTLE ITALY

A fine little stiff and stirred number from Audrey Saunders. Perfect for after dinner.

60 ml (2 fl oz) **rye whiskey**
15 ml (½ fl oz) **Cocchi sweet vermouth**
22 ml (¾ fl oz) **Cynar**
cherry, to garnish

Add all ingredients to a mixing glass with ice. Stir and strain into a frozen cocktail glass. Garnish with a cherry.

HEARTBREAKER COFFEE HOUSE

A tequila version of this caffeinated classic. This one has been bottled especially for Heartbreaker so no one has to wait to get their fix on a Saturday night.

45 ml (1½ fl oz) **tequila**
22 ml (¾ fl oz) **coffee liqueur**
2 dashes orange bitters
lemon twist, to garnish

Build ingredients in a rocks glass with ice. Garnish with a lemon twist.

STINGER

SIMILAR BUT DIFFERENT

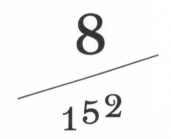

Style

'I am prepared to go anywhere, provided it be forward.'
   – David Livingstone,
      1813–1873

I remember so clearly the Sunday afternoon I received the call for my first host shift at Milk & Honey's sister bar, Little Branch. I needed a tie, a vest and suspenders for that evening. I ran to find whatever I could for the shift and from that day on, the way I dressed changed forever.

When it comes to style, confidence really is everything. You must wear your clothes, shoes and accessories with assurance and conviction, otherwise those efforts are wasted.

Dressing well made me reconsider the way I addressed and interacted with people. It gave me a new understanding of chivalry, manners and social etiquette. Feeling comfortable and confident improved my communication and my overall performance both behind and outside of the bar. It's no exaggeration to say that Milk & Honey and its policies made me a better person.

Function plays a vital role in the way we dress at The Everleigh. Customers are always asking how we manage to shake drinks all night without our shirts coming untucked, and we're happy to share our secrets. Although accents such as tie bars, headscarves and arm garters look fancy and fun, they wouldn't be there if they didn't have a job to do.

Just like our cocktails, our philosophy on how to dress revolves around function, quality and attention to detail. Here are a few tricks and tips to help you put your best foot forward, whatever the occasion.

HIS STYLE

Walk

Six classic shoe styles that have stood the test of time …

Oxford The Oxford gets straight As and is always invited back for a second interview. A confident and professional number named after the British university, the Oxford is a classic dress shoe, characterised by its closed lacing and eyelets attached under the vamp.

Originally cut a little smaller to give men a mincing step, the Oxford is a refined gent that excels in classic black leather. Posture is everything with this one. Keep the back straight by always having a shoehorn at the ready. That's right, that thing you used to fling rocks at your younger sibling with does have another use. And keep the polish close, old boy; this pair was born to shine.

Brogue (aka Wingtip) With daddy's credit card in his back pocket, the brogue is the master of extracurricular activity. He's charmed your mum, smoked cigars with your dad and should never be allowed near your sister.

This strong Celtic shoe was originally designed for country living, with distinctive perforations that allowed water to drain when crossing wet terrain. Though times have changed, this dapper lad is still breaking hearts in rich and robust tones.

Go on. Be fooled.

Monk strap Recently declared the most advanced dress shoe, the monk strap is fun, fancy and flamboyant. This moderately formal shoe has no lacing and is instead fastened with a buckle and strap.

Make it a double – step up your game with a double monk or even a triple strap ankle boot. This shoe is a showstopper. Buckle up – you're bound to have a great night.

Can't bare it? Don't be afraid to shun the sock. Pop an unvarnished cedar shoetree in each shoe between outings to eliminate unwanted odour and sweat.

Loafer In the late 1700s the term 'loafer' was used to describe an idle sailor who'd do anything to avoid hard work. This utterly convenient, all-purpose shoe allows you to slip out of the office and into the bar with elegance and ease.

Boot A thoroughly functional choice, the boot is your most loyal companion. By securing the foot well above the anklebone this reliable shoe will see you through a rough winter and lead you safely across uncharted territory.

A classic black, brown or even cordovan boot looks great with jeans for adventures, day or night. They also come in pretty handy around large spiders …

Sneaker No, not trainers, or runners. These guys wouldn't be seen dead in the gym. When it comes to sneakers you've got to kick back and roll your own. The canvas, suede or leather upper is a platform for your personality and nowadays it's safe to say there's a style for everyone.

In 1917, the United States Rubber Company began mass-producing the world's first sophisticated, comfortable rubber shoe. The nickname 'sneaker' came from how quietly it allowed one to travel on foot.

Did you know that the founders of Adidas and Puma were brothers? Unlike their mother it's ok to pick your favourite.

Complement

Suspenders Adding a little structured flair to a simple shirt and tie combo, suspenders allow you to adjust the height of your pants waist without having them appear as tight as they would with a belt.

Collar stiffeners To keep rogue collars from flaring up or curling under – a big Everleigh pet peeve.

Shirt stays How do we manage to shake drinks and run around all night without our shirts coming untucked? Mystery solved.

Pocket squares Much like your statement socks, the pocket square is the perfect way to add flair to a great outfit. Choose white and fold flat and sharp to form a break in your jacket, or go wild with colour.

Collar extenders For that great shirt you can't wear because it's a little too snug around the neck.

Tie bars Decorative? Yes, but also incredibly good at keeping your tie pinned to your shirt so it doesn't flap all over everyone when you bend over.

Arm garters A true gentleman wouldn't roll up his sleeves haphazardly. Avoid the whole affair by placing arm garters or sleeve suspenders around your biceps, which allow you to pin your cuffs up as high as they can go. Pull the sleeve up through the garter, leaving sleeve excess around your biceps.

Collars & ties – the perfect fit

Unsure what collar suits you best? Take a quick look in the mirror to see what face shape best describes you and check out our most complementary pairings below.

Collar vs. face shape
1 Angular faces are complemented by a wider spread collar.
2 Round faces are complemented by a narrow, pointed collar.
3 Oval faces are complemented by a medium spread collar.

Collar vs. knot No, that one knot you learnt at school isn't going to be enough. Here are the classic collar–knot combos for every occasion.
1 Classic narrow collar complemented by a Four In Hand
   Occasion: In the office
2 Button-down complemented by a Half Windsor
   Occasion: Night out with friends
3 Semi-spread complemented by a Half Windsor
   Occasion: Dinner date
4 Widespread collar complemented by a Double Windsor or Full Windsor
   Occasion: Cocktail party

HER STYLE

Walk

Six classic shoe styles that have stood the test of time ...

Pump A wardrobe staple from early adolescence, the pump is wise, worldly and continues to age with enviable grace. This shoe oozes versatility, varying dramatically in shape and style, from the structured high-heeled court shoe to soft, ballerina or dolly flats.

Classically characterised by a low-cut upper front and a lack of fastening, the pump is an international fashion favourite. Black or nude, suede or leather, patent or matte, pointed or rounded, wherever you're headed, be sure to have this pair in tow.

Wedge Packed full of height and style, the platform or wedge is the strong, confident and reliable type. An ancient Greek design that rose to fame in Italy in the late 1930s, the wedge sports a solid sole, much thicker at the back than the front, guaranteed to give you a lift.

Far from being a stick in the mud, this shoe is a practised professional when it comes to grassy ground – the perfect plus one for outdoor weddings and festivals.

Sandal Utterly self-assured without a hint of arrogance, the sandal is the ultimate laid-back babe of the shoe world – hell, you would be too if you spent that much time at the beach! Open-toed and all sole, this summer style aims to air it all out by leaving most of the upper foot exposed.

A 'barely-there' ankle-strap style in neutral tones goes with almost everything. For cooler climates or big cities, give a nod to the nineties with short-stacked heels and a peep toe with thick straps, offering height and coverage without sacrificing comfort.

As the sun goes down take it up a notch with sky-high heels, ideal for showing off those temporarily tanned pins.

Statement shoe Dare to flair with this pair. Bold, bright and beautiful, the statement shoe is the ultimate A-lister, show-stopping from toe to heel. A well-crafted pair will have eyes on your every move, so dig deep to win big.

Go wild with animal prints or take a shine to metallics. Allow for gloss, patterns, frills and feathers in a variety of materials and textures. Whatever you want to say, say it loud. We're listening.

Boot These boots are made for walking, and wherever they're going we call shotgun. Rugged and sexy, like a good whisk(e)y by a log fire, the boot is both functional and fashionable in every way.

Keen to keep it casual? Flat Chelsea boots or sleek ankle styles go great with jeans and dresses in any season. For the ultimate autumn look, try knee-length numbers in tan or brown, giving an elegant nod to equestrian style. And for maximum coverage and biker babe impact, take it thigh-high in matte black leather.

Sneaker From early morning coffee to late night adventures, the sneaker is a sociable sole that lives for the weekend. Clean-cut and fresh-faced, this shoe has no competition when it comes to comfort.

For an uber cool understated look, team casual kicks with structured formal wear or even more luxurious fabrics. No need to tread carefully here, mix and match with confidence to achieve sport luxe style that'll give anyone a run for their money.

Complement

The functional, fashionable role of a handbag is as old as time, but finding 'the one' that both looks great now and is certain to stick with you through the hard times is a difficult task. Here are a few hot tips for choosing a bag that's forever, not just for Christmas.

Is it …

Versatile? From day to night, from the office to dinner, an investment purchase such as this should be comfortable transitioning between occasions.

A shoulder strap is non-negotiable and ideally this one will be travel friendly – flexible enough to roll up and put in your suitcase where necessary.

Chic & functional? When deciding between styles, prioritise design details and functions according to your lifestyle. Do you value spaciousness, structure or comfort? Or features such as fringing, chains or buckles?

The winner will likely be a firm 50/50 split. A classic shape that elegantly incorporates essential functional features such as a strong, comfortable strap, plenty of pockets and secure fastenings.

A statement? Unlike the head-turning voluminous clutch that helps your friends spot you across a busy bar on a Saturday night, the 'Forever Bag' will be noticed time and time again for its understated beauty and classic sensibilities.

Keep it classy with black, oak, tan or grey. For a little extra attention consider patent or textured leathers (think croc-stamped or python) or even new neutrals and pastels – but beware of the upkeep!

Long-lasting? To have and to hold, from this day forward, for better, for worse, for richer, for poorer, in sickness and in health, until death do us part. It's called an investment purchase for a reason and should still see the light of day in 10–20 years to come, justifying that initial outlay.

Do your homework and invest in something that will last. Study the stitching throughout and look for a lining that's durable and easy to clean. A strong, smooth zipper is paramount, and feet on the bottom help to protect from wear and tear.

Opt for Saffiano leather and calfskin over suede. Lambskin is luxurious, sure, but it marks very easily.

Handbag essentials

Sure, she looks pretty under your arm but we all know it's what's inside that really counts. We've drawn up a little toolkit to make sure you're packing the good stuff whatever the weather.

The bare essentials …
Sunglasses *Daytime rock star*
Headphones *Hear me now*
Tissues *Soak it up*
Pen *Just sign here please …*

The quick fix …
Safety pins *You never know*
Band aids *Cut to the chase*
Extra earring backs *For the fallen ones*
Stain eraser pen *Nothing to see here*

The additional storage …
USB flash drive *On the download*
Portable phone charger *More juice please!*
Business card holder *Pocket professional*

The makeup magic …
Blotting papers *Don't sweat it*
Whitening eye drops *What hangover?*
Concealer/highlighter *Less bags, more cheekbone*
Hand cream *Pleased to meet you ooh!*
Lip balm *Pucker up*

$$\frac{9}{166}$$

Everleigh at Home

'Attractive, knowing service makes good
food taste superb.'

— *Esquire's Handbook for Hosts*, 1949

So you're throwing a party? How wonderful! Sure, there's some pressure involved. Who is going to show? What if there's not enough food? What music does everyone like? But with a little planning and preparation it is possible to pull this off seamlessly – and enjoy yourself too.

Hosting an event can be a scary experience. We understand. The host of a party is often the entertainer, server, chef and organiser all at once. Balancing all those duties requires dedication and care.

As anyone who has attended an Everleigh birthday party will tell you, we up the ante every year. We want to throw the best party Melbourne's seen, we want to raise a glass to everyone who loves us and, last but not least, we want to celebrate – and have some fun ourselves.

While it is undoubtedly a tricky task, it is possible to host an event and enjoy it yourself! This is the art of hosting.

Here are a few hints and tips for hosting a classic cocktail party at home, with love from The Everleigh. Just make sure our invitation doesn't get lost in the post …

THE COCKTAIL PARTY

How much for how many?

For the casual affair, void of formal invitations and RSVPs, count on about seventy per cent of those invited showing up. The smart host expects unexpected guests, and has an additional stash of liquor and snacks set aside.

With an average number of attendees in mind, you can calculate how many bottles of booze it'll take to keep everyone topped up throughout the evening. For example, a 700 ml (23½ fl oz) bottle of spirits will cater to approximately eleven cocktails. Depending what other beverages are on offer, it's wise to prepare for at least three cocktails per person.

Glassware & ice

When deciding on your menu for the evening, take note of which drinks go in which glass, (Collins glass, cocktail glass, rocks glass, etc.) and be sure to have enough of each shape and style. Stemmed cocktail glasses are guaranteed to do the rounds, taking care of your shaken citrusy numbers, stiff stirred classics and Champagne, should things get festive.

When it comes to ice, you always need more than you think. The DIY method is doable if you have the space, time and enthusiasm. Alternatively, order hand-cut blocks from your nearest ice company and wow the crowd with diamond cuts they can read a book through.

Light fare

Serving some light fare alongside your welcome drink will help put guests at ease. Single-mouthful–size snacks are ideal. Present these on sharing plates to keep things social, but make sure they're not too large, or else food will be left to go stale.

Setting the tone

Inviting people into your home is a generous, hospitable act. Whether humble or lavish, it's your home, and it's a place you should be proud of. That said, in preparation for hosting it is always wise to consider what you'd like your guests to learn about you and what might best be kept private.

In the calm air of the afternoon, before things get busy, note any embarrassing, unsavoury or incriminating items and see that they are stashed safely out of sight. Don't assume that new colleague you've been getting on so well with will know that *The Book of Big Breasts* was a Secret Santa gift and, unless you want your success with laser hair removal to be a topic of conversation, it'd be wise to take your appointment reminder card off the fridge.

In terms of décor, take this opportunity to flaunt your favourite things. Framed photographs and curious ornaments are charming, and assist with the recounting of worldly tales. Fill the room with fresh flowers and plenty of candles, keeping electric lighting at a moody low. Appear cultured with a playlist that's neither generic nor wildly adventurous. Unless you're hosting a karaoke party, be sure to lower volume levels well before guests are expected. The same goes for later in the evening. That song might sound amazing to you at 3 am but, as unreasonable as it may seem, your neighbours are unlikely to agree …

Social etiquette

To avoid boring the first to arrive with your disappointment that the soufflé didn't quite turn out the way it did last time, brush up on topical events likely to spark light and interesting conversation. Prepare to conduct guest introductions with confidence by triple-checking the names of your colleagues' partners. Stalk social media profiles where necessary, but be sure to act surprised when the person shows you their new tattoo, tells you about their recent holiday, or shares their controversial views on climate change.

The chores always take longer than you expect and, regardless of clear instructions, someone always arrives a little early. There's no excuse to answer the door in your robe. Get the heavy cleaning out of the way and then get dressed. It's a good idea to wear something cool, regardless of the season, as there's likely to be some last-minute running around to do.

It's been a long day and you've worked hard. Treat yourself to a beer while you're getting ready, but just the one. You want to be sober enough to entertain, but merry enough to be entertaining.

LIGHT FARE

Here are some classic tidbits that have got us out of a tight (hungry and tipsy) spot when hosting soirées over the years. Many have also appeared on canapé menus for cocktail parties in The Everleigh's private bar, The Elk Room.

The main aim here is to complement your cocktails and garner compliments from your guests. Each dish is simple, effective and requires minimal preparation. Serve early to curb any hunger pangs inspired by your welcome drink, and plan for leftovers to nibble later, with your nightcap.

BUTTER RADISHES

Makes 16

16 baby radishes with leafy tops
225 g (8 oz) unsalted butter, at room temperature
1¼ tablespoons sea salt (fleur de sel, if possible)

Wash your radishes in cool water, removing any dirt. Pat dry, then slice the bottoms off the radishes so they sit flat. Warm the butter slowly in a bowl over a saucepan of water on the stove. Alternatively, microwave the butter in 4-second intervals, whisking in between, until it has the consistency of melted chocolate.

Dip the lower half of the radishes into the butter once or twice until well coated. Shake to remove excess butter, then place on wax paper and refrigerate until the butter is set. Season with sea salt to taste.

CRAB TOASTS

Makes 20 (approx.)

125 g (4½ oz/½ cup) mayonnaise
half a loaf of sourdough, sliced
340 g (12 oz) crabmeat
45 g (1½ oz/¼ cup) capers, rinsed and squeezed dry
1 teaspoon red chilli flakes
60 ml (2 fl oz/¼ cup) extra-virgin olive oil
zest and juice of 2 lemons
sea salt and freshly ground black pepper, to taste

Heat a cast-iron grill pan over a high heat. Spread mayonnaise on both sides of each slice of bread and season with salt. Grill the bread for about 4–5 minutes, flipping once, until slightly charred and crisp. Place the toast on a serving platter. Combine all your other ingredients in a bowl, then spoon onto each piece of toast and spread evenly. Slice the toast into triangular thirds and serve.

DEVILLED EGGS

Makes 24

12 large eggs, at room
  temperature
6 tablespoons mayonnaise
2 tablespoons crème fraîche
2 teaspoons dijon mustard
2 tablespoons Champagne
  vinegar
sea salt
2 tablespoons finely chopped
  chervil
4 tablespoons finely chopped
  chives
cayenne pepper or paprika,
  to dust

Place a pan of water on a high heat and bring to the boil.
Lower the eggs into the water gently and cook for 10
minutes. Drain the eggs and place in a bowl of iced water
until cool. Peel the eggs, then halve lengthways and scoop out
the yolks. Set the whites aside, then push the yolks through a
strainer or sieve into a bowl. Add mayonnaise, crème fraîche,
mustard and vinegar and stir until smooth. Season with sea salt
to taste. Chill the mixture in the fridge for 30 minutes, along
with the cooked egg whites wrapped or covered in plastic wrap.
Once chilled, pat the egg whites dry and pipe the yolk mixture
onto the whites. Sprinkle with chervil, chives and a dusting of
cayenne pepper or paprika to finish*.

*   *Add a dollop of caviar on top to get the ever-so-fancy* **Uptown Devilled
    Eggs***.*

DEVILS ON HORSEBACK

Makes 20

20 pitted prunes*
40 g (1½ oz) blue cheese,
  cut into 20 small chunks
10 rashers bacon, halved
  lengthways (use prosciutto
  or pancetta if you prefer)

Preheat the oven to 220°C (430°F). Soak the prunes in warm
water for 15 minutes, then drain and pat dry with paper towel.
Push a chunk of blue cheese into the centre of each prune
before wrapping it with half a slice of bacon. Secure each prune
with a toothpick and bake on an oven tray for approximately
10 minutes, until the bacon is crispy. Transfer to paper towels to
drain excess fat and leave to stand for 5 minutes before serving.

*   *For* **Angels on Horseback***, swap prunes for oysters and hold the cheese. Season
    with cayenne pepper and fresh lemon to serve.*

STUFFED GREEN OLIVES

Makes 30

113 g (4 oz) Italian sausage,
  casing removed
2 tablespoons grated parmesan
  cheese
1 garlic clove (pressed)
1½ teaspoons freshly chopped
  parsley
½ teaspoon lemon zest
½ teaspoon dried chilli flakes
30 large green Italian olives,
  pitted
40 g (1½ oz/¾ cup) panko
  crumbs (finely ground)
75 g (2¾ oz/½ cup) plain flour
1 large egg
vegetable oil (for frying)
sea salt and freshly ground
  black pepper

Mix the sausage, parmesan, garlic, parsley, lemon zest, chilli flakes and a big pinch of salt and pepper together in a bowl. Cut a small slit lengthways down the side of each olive, then stuff with the sausage mixture, pressing gently to seal. Sprinkle ¼ cup of ground panko crumbs onto a rimmed baking sheet and set aside. Place the remaining panko crumbs, flour and egg in three separate shallow bowls. Add 1 teaspoon of water to the egg and whisk.
Taking a handful of olives at a time, place first in the flour to coat, then in the beaten egg, and finally in the panko. Shake off any excess and place the crumbed olives on the baking sheet. Cover with plastic wrap and chill in the fridge for approximately 30 minutes.
Heat enough oil for deep-frying in a saucepan over a medium heat. Once the oil is hot enough that a breadcrumb sizzles on contact, deep-fry the olives in small batches. Fry, stirring occasionally, for about 7 minutes, or until the olives are golden and the sausage filling is cooked. Drain on paper towels and allow to cool slightly before serving.

WELSH RAREBIT

Makes 16

50 g (1¾ oz) unsalted butter
3 tablespoons flour
150 ml (5 fl oz) strong ale
worcestershire sauce, to taste
1 heaped teaspoon dijon
  mustard
200 g (7 oz) vintage cheddar,
  grated
4 large slices rustic bread
sea salt and freshly ground
  black pepper

Preheat the grill (broiler) to a medium heat. Melt the butter in a small saucepan, then add the flour and mix well. Cook for 2–3 minutes, stirring continuously until the flour has cooked out and the texture is smooth, then slowly add the ale, mixing well. Remove the mixture from the heat, then add the worcestershire sauce and mustard, and mix again. Add three-quarters of the cheddar and stir until the cheese has completely melted, then set the mixture aside to cool.
Toast the bread under the grill (broiler) until golden on each side, then place on a baking tray and spread the cheese mixture across each slice to the very edges. Top with the remaining cheese, a little more worcestershire, salt and pepper and cook under the grill until dark golden and bubbling. Slice each piece of toast into quarters and allow to cool slightly before serving.

THE FOUR ACES

For us, 'classic cocktail' means a timeless, elegant drink, simple in style and form and premium in quality. Cocktails of this calibre are bold and proud in flavour and appearance. We show them the respect they deserve by always using the finest and freshest ingredients we can get our hands on.

The beauty of the four aces lies in their simplicity. Each drink in the set is quick and easy to prepare, yet packs a punch. Whether it's an aperitif or a nightcap you're after, the four aces cover all bases.

The Everleigh Bottling Co. was created to offer those who love our drinks the opportunity to enjoy their favourite cocktails at home, prepared to the exact same standard of those ordered over the bar. While there are so many classic cocktails to choose from, we believe that these are the four that come up trumps time and time again.

Sure, they've been around a while, but there's a reason we're still drinking them. Instead of lagging behind in the contemporary cocktail race, these age-old legends remain at the top of their game.

The only real question is, which one are we having first?

THE MARTINI

60 ml (2 fl oz) **gin**
30 ml (1 fl oz) **Dolin dry vermouth**
2 dashes **orange bitters**
olive, pickled onion or lemon twist, to garnish

Add your ingredients to a mixing glass with ice. Stir and strain into a frozen cocktail glass. Garnish with a lemon twist, an olive or a pickled onion.

*Big fan of Scotch whisky? Before straining your Martini into the glass, rinse it with a little Scotch whisky and you have the **Smoky Martini**. Garnish with a lemon twist.*

*Got some sherry in the fridge? Take our house Martini and swap out the dry vermouth for dry sherry to get the **Tuxedo #1**. Again, this one needs a lemon twist to garnish.*

*Like to keep it pretty clean but keen for a little something extra? The **Blenton** is a classic Martini with three dashes of Angostura bitters, garnished with a lemon twist.*

*What about something sweeter? Take our classic 2:1 ratio and simply switch out the dry vermouth for Cocchi Americano to get the **Richmond**, a golden oldie from 1934. Garnish this one with a lemon twist.*

*Never tried a Martini with sweet vermouth? You don't know what you're missing! Go equal parts sweet vermouth and gin with a dash of maraschino liqueur and a few dashes of orange bitters and you have the **Martinez**.*

The origins of the Martini are shrouded in mystery; everyone wants a piece of her. Described by author H.L. Mencken as 'the only American invention as perfect as the sonnet', the Martini is so strong and sexy, simply ordering one is enough to make us weak at the knees.

*This 2:1 ratio is our house Martini (2 parts gin to 1 part dry vermouth). We love it quite 'wet', which is to say we like it with more dry vermouth. If you like it even more wet, try the **Fifty Fifty**, which is equal parts gin and vermouth.*

If dry is more your style, the 5:1 ratio should do the trick – 5 parts gin to 1 part dry vermouth. That's 75 ml (2½ fl oz) gin to 15 ml (½ fl oz) dry vermouth.

*Like it dirty? How dirty? We use the terms dusty, dirty and filthy to describe the varying levels of olive brine desired. For a **Dusty Martini** add 7 ml (¼ fl oz), for a **Dirty Martini** add 15 ml (½ fl oz) and for a full throttle **Filthy Martini** throw in 22 ml (¾ fl oz).*

Go crazy with those olive garnishes. We pop one in the drink and two in a sidecar.

*Like yours garnished with a pickled onion? We call that a **Gibson**. The possibilities are almost endless.*

DEEP BLUE SEA

This cocktail was the first drink I ever worked on with Sasha. We played with so many different versions before settling on this one and it was worth the effort. I still think this drink is damn fine.

60 ml (2 fl oz) **gin**
22 ml (¾ fl oz) **Cocchi Americano**
7 ml (¼ fl oz) **violet liqueur**
2 dashes **orange bitters**
lemon twist, to garnish

Add your ingredients to a mixing glass with ice. Stir and strain into a frozen cocktail glass. Garnish with a lemon twist.

POET'S DREAM

60 ml (2 fl oz) **gin**
22 ml (¾ fl oz) **Dolin dry vermouth**
7 ml (¼ fl oz) **Benedictine**
2 dashes **orange bitters**
lemon twist, to garnish

Add your ingredients to a mixing glass with ice. Stir and strain into a frozen cocktail glass. Garnish with a lemon twist.

ROLLS ROYCE

This classy but shady gent has a couple of known aliases. You may hear him referred to as the Football Hero or Lamb's Club.

60 ml (2 fl oz) **gin**
15 ml (½ fl oz) **Dolin dry vermouth**

Add a few dashes of orange bitters and you have a subtle variation called the __Zimmy__.

Switch Benedictine out for yellow Chartreuse and you've got yourself a __Puritan__. This variation brings a really herbaceous quality to the drink. We recommend a light, dry vermouth such as Dolin from Chambéry.

This one's the Milk & Honey take on a drink made famous by Ian Fleming's James Bond.

15 ml (½ fl oz) **Cocchi sweet vermouth**
1 dash (5 ml) **Benedictine**
lemon twist, to garnish

Add your ingredients to a mixing glass with ice. Stir and strain into a frozen cocktail glass. Garnish with a lemon twist.

TUXEDO #2

The tux #2 is one of the number one Martini variations.

60 ml (2 fl oz) **gin**
22 ml (¾ fl oz) **Dolin dry vermouth**
7 ml (¼ fl oz) **maraschino liqueur**
2 dashes **absinthe**
2 dashes **orange bitters**
lemon twist and a cherry, to garnish

Add your ingredients to a mixing glass with ice. Stir and strain into a frozen cocktail glass. Garnish with a lemon twist and a cherry.

VESPER

60 ml (2 fl oz) **gin**
15 ml (½ fl oz) **vodka**
15 ml (½ fl oz) **Cocchi Americano**
lemon twist, to garnish

Add your ingredients to a mixing glass with ice. Stir and strain into a frozen cocktail glass. Garnish with a lemon twist.

THE NEGRONI

22 ml (¾ fl oz) **gin**
30 ml (1 fl oz) **Cocchi sweet vermouth**
22 ml (¾ fl oz) **Campari**
orange twist, to garnish

Build your ingredients in a rocks glass with ice. Garnish with an orange twist.

Add a few dashes of absinthe to get one of my personal favourites, the **Quill**.

Top up your Negroni with a splash of sparkling wine and you've got the **Famiglia Reale**.

Take the gin out completely and replace it with sparkling wine for the low-alcohol, bubbly aperitif **Negroni S'bagliato**. *Champagne will of course also do nicely in both cases!*

Our Negroni is Melbourne's favourite back-pocket cocktail. Utilising Cocchi sweet vermouth to a carefully considered degree, we created what was described by Drinks International as 'one of the best we've ever had. Anywhere. Ever.' in the coveted *World's Top 50 Bars*, 2013.

CAMPARINETTE

Like this, only different … Tiki Godfather, Trader Vic delivered this to us in his *Bartender's Guide* back in 1947. Be sure to say this one with your hands, like they do in eee-taly.

60 ml (2 fl oz) **gin**
15 ml (½ fl oz) **Cocchi sweet vermouth**
15 ml (½ fl oz) **Campari**
orange twist, to garnish

Add your ingredients to a mixing glass with ice. Stir and strain into a frozen cocktail glass. Garnish with an orange twist.

JOHN PERONA

Ted Saucier featured this one in his saucily named 1951 collection, *Bottoms Up.* He made this drink for a friend of his, said to be the king of the 1930s New York nightclub scene. It's definitely enough to get us dancing.

45 ml (1½ fl oz) **gin**
37 ml (1¼ fl oz) **Cocchi sweet vermouth**
1 dash (5 ml) **Campari**
lemon twist, to garnish

Add your ingredients to a mixing glass with ice. Stir and strain into a frozen cocktail glass. Garnish with a lemon twist.

*Swap your gin for tequila for a flirty number called **La Rosita** (remember to roll your r's when serving).*

TUNNEL (AKA THE FASCINATOR)

Two names, yes. Many classic drinks are known by a number of names. Remember, recipes were recorded on anything from napkins to matchbooks to backs of hands, and those doing the writing were probably drunk. Tunnel was the first recorded name, in 1937, but we prefer Fascinator as it reminds us of those ridiculous hats people wear at weddings and the races.

45 ml (1½ fl oz) **gin**
15 ml (½ fl oz) **Dolin dry vermouth**
15 ml (½ fl oz) **Cocchi sweet vermouth**
15 ml (½ fl oz) **Campari**
lemon twist, to garnish

Add your ingredients to a mixing glass with ice. Stir and strain into a frozen cocktail glass. Garnish with a lemon twist.

GLORIA

Another winner from Trader Vic back in 1947.

45 ml (1½ fl oz) **gin**
15 ml (½ fl oz) **Campari**
15 ml (½ fl oz) **Dolin dry vermouth**
15 ml (½ fl oz) **Cointreau**
lemon twist, to garnish

Add your ingredients to a mixing glass with ice. Stir and strain into a frozen cocktail glass. Garnish with a lemon twist.

THE MANHATTAN

60 ml (2 fl oz) **rye whiskey**
30 ml (1 fl oz) **Cocchi sweet vermouth**
cherry, to garnish

Add your ingredients to a mixing glass with ice. Stir and strain into a frozen cocktail glass. Garnish with a cherry.

Manhattan Junior just requires an orange twist in place of a cherry garnish. This is a really great, incredibly simple twist.

Need a little spice? The <u>Meteor</u> is a classic Manhattan with a dash of absinthe.

Sweet tooth? Add a dash of maple syrup to get a drink called the <u>Habitant</u>.

Don't have rye? Don't sweat. Bourbon works nicely too. Add a dash of absinthe to your bourbon Manhattan and you have the <u>Waldorf</u>.

Feel like mixing it up even more? Cut your rye in half and replace with Cognac so you have equal parts, for the <u>Saratoga</u>.

An elegant, boozy cocktail that dates back to the 1870s. Rich in vermouth flavour and rye whiskey.

Rye, bourbon's spicier sibling, is the original whiskey used to make the Manhattan, and this one packs a punch at 45% abv. Our bottled Manhattan is our favourite of the four.

DE LA LOUISIANE

60 ml (2 fl oz) **rye whiskey**

15 ml (½ fl oz) **Cocchi sweet vermouth**

15 ml (½ fl oz) **Benedictine**

2 dashes **Peychaud's bitters**

2 dashes **absinthe**

lemon twist, to garnish

Add your ingredients to a mixing glass with ice. Stir and strain into a frozen cocktail glass. Garnish with a lemon twist.

PREAKNESS

60 ml (2 fl oz) **rye whiskey**

22 ml (¾ fl oz) **Cocchi sweet vermouth**

7 ml (¼ fl oz) **Benedictine**

3 dashes **Angostura bitters**

lemon twist, to garnish

Add your ingredients to a mixing glass with ice. Stir and strain into a frozen cocktail glass. Garnish with a lemon twist.

HOLLOW POINT

A customer told us about a drink named Hollow Point that he'd tried. We didn't know it but asked if we could give it a shot. He rattled off a few ingredients and we threw them all together. The result was pure magic.

45 ml (1½ fl oz) **bourbon**

15 ml (½ fl oz) **Cocchi sweet vermouth**

11 ml (⅜ fl oz) **apricot liqueur**

11 ml (⅜ fl oz) **Campari**

lemon twist, to garnish

Add a little dash of absinthe to get the __Cotton Cocktail__.

This variation on the Manhattan is like a Sazerac on steroids.

Add your ingredients to a mixing glass with ice. Stir and strain into a frozen cocktail glass. Garnish with a lemon twist.

1920 COCKTAIL

60 ml (2 fl oz) **rye whiskey**

15 ml (½ fl oz) **Cocchi sweet vermouth**

15 ml (½ fl oz) **Dolin dry vermouth**

2 dashes **Angostura bitters**

2 dashes **orange bitters**

lemon twist, to garnish

Add your ingredients to a mixing glass with ice. Stir and strain into a frozen cocktail glass. Garnish with a lemon twist.

BLUE COLLAR COCKTAIL

This drink was born when I accidentally mixed up the recipe for a Brooklyn with that of a Liberal. We've been accidentally on purpose making it this way ever since.

60 ml (2 fl oz) **rye whiskey**

15 ml (½ fl oz) **Cocchi sweet vermouth**

7 ml (¼ fl oz) **Amer Picon**

7 ml (¼ fl oz) **maraschino liqueur**

2 dashes **Angostura bitters**

2 dashes **orange bitters**

lemon twist, to garnish

Add your ingredients to a mixing glass with ice. Stir and strain into a frozen cocktail glass.Garnish with a lemon twist.

THE OLD FASHIONED

60 ml (2 fl oz) **bourbon**
3 dashes Angostura bitters
1 white sugar cube
1 bar spoon soda
orange and lemon twists,
 to garnish

Add all ingredients except bourbon to a rocks glass. Crush the sugar cube with a muddler and add bourbon. Add ice and spin the glass once or twice. Garnish with an orange and a lemon twist.

*Like many of the drinks in this book, there are many variations on the classics. The simplest variation on the Old Fashioned is the **Hendrick**, which calls for a dash of absinthe.*

*If you prefer Scotch whisky over bourbon, try the **Choker**, a Scotch Old Fashioned with a dash of absinthe. Zara likes hers with a dash of peaty whisky too. She calls that one the **Smoky Choker**.*

There are many ways to make this drink. Its simplicity means it's even more important to get it right. Our version is what we call the *Old* Old Fashioned. No salad, no overdilution. Just whiskey, bitters and sugar over ice.

IMPROVED WHISKEY COCKTAIL

60 ml (2 fl oz) rye whiskey
15 ml (½ fl oz) maraschino
liqueur
2 dashes Peychaud's bitters
2 dashes absinthe
lemon twist, to garnish

Build in a rocks glass with ice.
Garnish with a lemon twist.

TALENT SCOUT

60 ml (2 fl oz) bourbon
15 ml (½ fl oz) orange curaçao
3 dashes Angostura bitters
lemon twist, to garnish

Build in a rocks glass with ice.
Garnish with a lemon twist.

ALCAZAR

60 ml (2 fl oz) rye whiskey
15 ml (½ fl oz) Benedictine
2 dashes orange bitters
lemon twist, to garnish

Build in a rocks glass with ice.
Garnish with a lemon twist.

BEE KEEPER

60 ml (2 fl oz) bourbon
1 bar spoon honey syrup
3 dashes Angostura bitters
2 dashes absinthe
lemon twist, to garnish

Build in a rocks glass with ice.
Garnish with a lemon twist.

Swap the bourbon for rye and you have the Approve Cocktail.

Swap orange bitters for Angostura and you've got the Monte Carlo.

MARDIS GRAS

60 ml (2 fl oz) rye whiskey
2 dashes Peychaud's bitters
2 dashes Angostura bitters
3 dashes absinthe
1 white sugar cube
1 bar spoon soda water
lemon twist, to garnish

Add all ingredients except
the rye whiskey to a rocks glass.
Crush the sugar cube with a
muddler and add the rye. Add
ice and spin the glass once or
twice. Garnish with a lemon
twist.

KENTUCKY RIVER (AKA FOX RIVER)

60 ml (2 fl oz) bourbon
15 ml (½ fl oz) crème de cacao
2 dashes peach bitters
lemon twist, to garnish

Build in a rocks glass with ice.
Garnish with a lemon twist.

BEE BEE

60 ml (2 fl oz) bourbon
15 ml (½ fl oz) honey syrup
3 dashes Angostura bitters
3 lemon twists
3 orange twists

Add twists to a rocks glass
with honey syrup and bitters.
Press the skins firmly with a
muddler to release the oils.
Add bourbon and ice and mix
with a spoon.

THE OLD FASHIONED

SIMILAR BUT DIFFERENT

THE EVERLEIGH
BOTTLING C⁰

MANHATTAN

MANUFACTURED TO THE
MOST EXACTING STANDARDS
UPSTAIRS 150 GERTRUDE STR.
FITZROY VICTORIA 3065

PUNCHES

There's something fun and innocent about sharing a drink. No, we're not talking about the stingy 'there are three of us, but we're only going to have one sip each' scenario. We're referring to that seemingly endless supply of boozy goodness that got everyone giddy at your last garden party.

To avoid being bowled over by just one glass, follow a simple recipe and measure your ingredients. Get the proportions right to begin with and you'll have everyone coming back for more. What the guests top it up with when your head is turned is tomorrow morning's worry …

FISH HOUSE PUNCH

(serves 10–12)

Bold and boozy – Now that'll get the party started …

350 ml (12 fl oz) **Cognac**
255 ml (8½ fl oz) **Jamaican dark rum**
255 ml (8½ fl oz) **lemon juice**
255 ml (8½ fl oz) **peach brandy or liqueur**
255 ml (8½ fl oz) **filtered water**
lemon, orange and peach slices, to garnish

Add all the ingredients to a punchbowl with large blocks of ice. Stir, then garnish with slices of lemon, orange and peach. Serve in a rocks glass with ice.

MINT PUNCH

(serves 10–12)

This one's perfect for a hot summer's day with friends. It's like a Mint Julep on steroids! If you have the time, leave the mint to infuse in the sugar syrup for a couple of hours before making the punch. That way, when you add it to the mixture, the flavour will spread throughout the drink more evenly.

700 ml (23½ fl oz) **bourbon**
350 ml (12 fl oz) **lime juice**
265 ml (9 fl oz) **mint syrup (see below)**
500 ml (17 fl oz) **soda**
absinthe, to taste

fresh mint and lime slices, to garnish
For the mint syrup:
handful mint leaves
265 ml (9 fl oz) **sugar syrup**

Add all ingredients except the absinthe to a punchbowl with large blocks of ice. Stir before adding a touch of absinthe to taste – not enough to overpower the other flavours, but just enough for a little refreshing spice. Serve in a rocks glass with ice.

PISCO PUNCH

(serves 10–12)

The day before serving, steep chopped pineapple in sugar syrup overnight. Remember, the syrup will only keep for a couple of days, so don't make too much. Strain the syrup before using.

700 ml (23½ fl oz) **pisco brandy**
300 ml (10 fl oz) **pineapple syrup (see below)**
300 ml (10 fl oz) **lemon juice**
500 ml (17 fl oz) **filtered water**
fresh pineapple slices, to garnish
For the pineapple syrup:
½ **pineapple, cut into 2 cm (¾ in) cubes**
300 ml (10 fl oz) **sugar syrup**

Add all the ingredients to a punchbowl with large blocks of ice. Stir and garnish with fresh pineapple slices. Serve in a rocks glass with ice.

Must be prepared 1 day prior

FRUIT CUP PUNCH

(serves 10–12)

The perfect recipe for home-
made Pimm's.

175 ml (6 fl oz) **gin**
175 ml (6 fl oz) **Cocchi sweet
vermouth**
90 ml (3 fl oz) **Grand Marnier**
60 ml (2 fl oz) **Cherry Heering**
**sliced oranges, lemons,
limes, mint, cucumber and
seasonal berries**
**approx. 700 ml–1 L
(23½–34 fl oz) lemonade,
soda or ginger beer**

Add gin, vermouth,
Grand Marnier and cherry
liqueur to a punchbowl with
large blocks of ice. Go wild
with a generous amount of
sliced citrus, mint, cucumber
and seasonal berries. Top it up
with lemonade, soda or ginger
beer as you see fit. Feel free to
add extra soda if required –
this one is intended to be a
fairly light drink, not too boozy.
Serve in a rocks glass with ice.

INVISIBLE GIN PUNCH

(serves 10–12)

700 ml (23½ fl oz) **gin**
450 ml (15 fl oz) **fresh
pineapple juice**
240 ml (8 fl oz) **lemon juice**
500–700 ml (17–23½ fl oz)
ginger beer
**pineapple and lemon slices,
to garnish**

Add gin, pineapple juice and
lemon juice to a punchbowl
with large blocks of ice. Top up
with ginger beer to taste.
Garnish with pineapple and
lemon slices. Serve in a rocks
glass with ice.

BOURBON MILK PUNCH

(serves 10–12)

Here's a hearty number, perfect
for winter lunches.

450 ml (15 fl oz) **bourbon**
180 ml (6 fl oz) **aged dark rum**
720 ml (24 fl oz) **full cream
milk**
180 ml (6 fl oz) **sugar syrup**
45 ml (1½ fl oz) **vanilla extract**
**freshly grated nutmeg, to
garnish**

Add all ingredients to a
punchbowl with large blocks
of ice. Stir, then garnish with
freshly grated nutmeg. Serve
in a rocks glass with ice and
garnish each drink again with
more grated nutmeg.

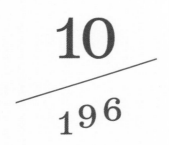

Nightcaps

'Recalling certain gentlemen of other days, who made of drinking one of the pleasures of life – not one of its evils; who achieved content lone ere capacity was reached or overtaxed; and who, whatever they drank, proved able to carry it, keep their heads and remain gentlemen, even in their cups. Their example is commended to their posterity.'

– Albert Stevens Crockett,
   The Old Waldorf Astoria Bar Book, 1935

What a night. This has certainly been one to remember. So good, in fact, that you have long surpassed that 'I've got lots on tomorrow' curfew. Your eyelids are getting heavy, but the conversation is still flowing, so you've agreed to just one more …

Make sure this last one really hits the spot. It doesn't have to be strong, but it should definitely be tasty.

Here's a tipple or two we think cap off the night just right.

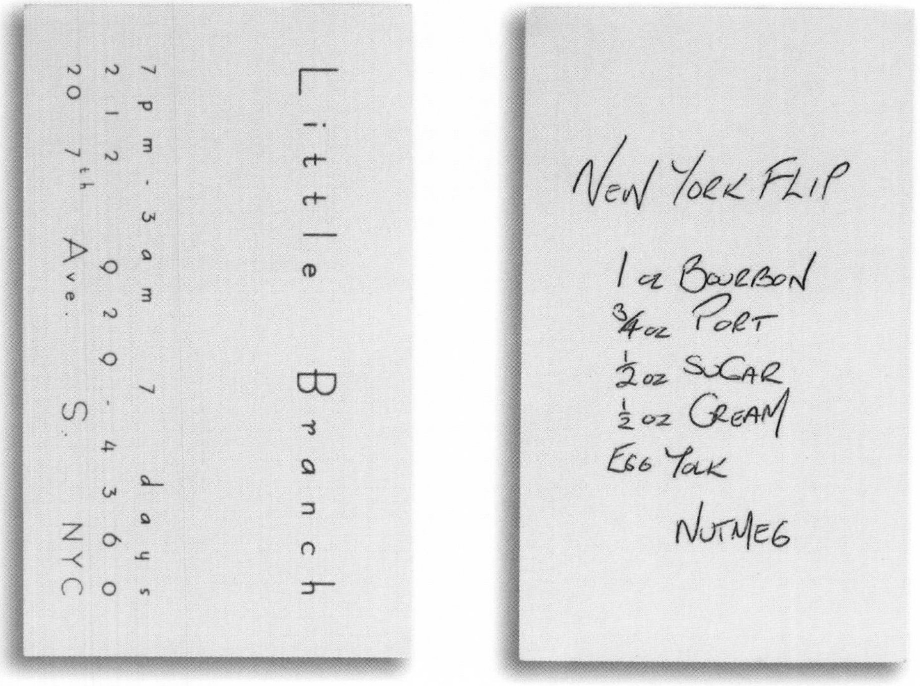

Little Branch

7pm - 3am 7 days
212 929.4360
20 7th Ave. S. NYC

New York Flip

1 oz Bourbon
3/4 oz Port
1/2 oz Sugar
1/2 oz Cream
Egg Yolk

Nutmeg

NEW YORK FLIP

30 ml (1 fl oz) **bourbon**
22 ml (¾ fl oz) **tawny Port**
15 ml (½ fl oz) **sugar syrup**
15 ml (½ fl oz) **cream**
1 **egg yolk**
freshly grated nutmeg,
  to garnish

Add all ingredients except
egg yolk to a shaker. Add the egg
yolk and dry shake to emulsify.
Add ice and shake hard.
Strain into a frozen cocktail
glass and garnish with freshly
grated nutmeg.

*Replace the sugar with honey to get
the **East New York Flip**.*

*Prefer Scotch whisky? A straight swap with
the bourbon will get you the **Morning Star**.*

*Opt for a base of apple brandy instead and
you have the **Lazy Man Flip**.*

*Make it Cognac and you'll be drinking
a **Charlestown Bracer**.*

I wish I could have seen my expression
the first time I tried this drink.
I remember it well, I was goddamn
impressed. The New York Flip is rich,
booze-driven and creamy in equal
measure; the perfect bedtime treat.

COFFEE COCKTAIL

45 ml (1½ fl oz) **Cognac**
45 ml (1½ fl oz) **tawny Port**
7 ml (¼ fl oz) **sugar syrup**
1 whole **egg**
freshly grated **nutmeg**, to
    garnish

Add all ingredients except the
egg to a shaker. Add the egg and
dry shake to emulsify. Add ice
and shake hard. Strain into a
frozen cocktail glass and garnish
with freshly grated nutmeg.

*This one appeared in the
1887 edition of the world's
first cocktail book, A
Bartender's Guide, by Jerry
Thomas. There's no coffee,
but it's still delicious.*

SILVER FOX

Invented by a man with an
enviable head of hair, Mr Richard
Boccato of Dutch Kills, NYC.

45 ml (1½ fl oz) **gin**
22 ml (¾ fl oz) **lemon juice**
15 ml (½ fl oz) **orgeat**
7 ml (¼ fl oz) **amaretto**
1 **egg white**
soda

Add all ingredients except egg
white and soda to a shaker. Add
the egg white and dry shake to
emulsify. Add ice and shake
hard. Strain into a frozen fizz
glass and top with soda.

*Use aged dark rum in place
of Scotch whisky if you
prefer, to make one of mine
from the PDT days called
The Professor.*

ATHOL BROSE

60 ml (2 fl oz) **single malt
    Scotch whisky**
22 ml (¾ fl oz) **honey syrup**
hand-whipped cream

Add Scotch whisky and honey
syrup to a mixing glass with
ice. Stir and strain into a frozen

*If you have a little Islay whisky
at hand, an additional splash
certainly won't go amiss.*

cocktail glass. Float your hand-
whipped cream on top.

N
E
W

Y
O
R
K

F
L
I
P

VIEUX CARRÉ

This one hails from one of the
greatest cities in the world,
New Orleans, and is named
after the city's French quarter.

22 ml (¾ fl oz) **rye whiskey**
22 ml (¾ fl oz) **Cognac**
30 ml (1 fl oz) **Cocchi
    sweet vermouth**
1 dash (5 ml) **Benedictine**
2 dashes **Angostura bitters**
2 dashes **Peychaud's bitters**
cherry and a **lemon twist**,
    to garnish

Build all ingredients in a rocks
glass with ice. Garnish with a
cherry and a lemon twist.

CHANCELLOR #2

The original Chancellor #1
used dry vermouth in place
of sweet, but Joseph Schwartz
of Little Branch, NYC, switched
them around for our menu one
year. It went down a treat.

45 ml (1½ fl oz) **Scotch whisky**
30 ml (1 fl oz) **tawny Port**
15 ml (½ fl oz) **Cocchi sweet
    vermouth**
2 dashes **Angostura bitters**
cherry, to garnish

Add all ingredients to a mixing
glass with ice. Stir and strain
into a frozen cocktail glass.
Garnish with a cherry.

S
I
M
I
L
A
R

B
U
T

D
I
F
F
E
R
E
N
T

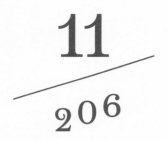

$$\frac{11}{206}$$

The Morning After

So, last night was great, right? You got to catch up with friends you've not seen in an age. Most significantly, you managed to forget about all the stuff you've been tearing your hair out over and simply enjoyed yourself.

Hungover? Sure, it happens. And yes, it was worth it. In the spirit of living, don't start the day with a sour (okay, outright foul) taste in your mouth. Instead, let's focus on what we can do this morning to make you feel half as fantastic as you did when you ordered that last round of shots at 3 am …

Someone might have told you that it's a good idea to consume plenty of water while drinking. Essentially, your body needs both hydration and sleep to recover, but seeing as your mates are determined to enjoy a sunny Saturday, we'd better get you in the shower and whip up a little hair of the dog.

THE MARMALADE
COCKTAIL

2oz GIN
3/4oz LEMON
3/4oz MARMALADE SYRUP

MARMALADE COCKTAIL

60 ml (2 fl oz) **gin**
22 ml (¾ fl oz) **lemon juice**
22 ml (¾ fl oz) **marmalade
  syrup**

Add all ingredients to a shaker.
Mix well, add ice and shake.
Strain into a frozen cocktail
glass.

*Don't like marmalade? Replace with
a heaped bar spoon of raspberry
preserve to get the **Cosmonaut**,
one of Sasha's old favourites.*

'By its bittersweet taste,
this cocktail is especially suited
to be a luncheon aperitif.'

  – Harry Craddock,
  The Savoy Cocktail Book, 1930

Cut the toast and head straight to
the sauce …

CORPSE REVIVER #2

22 ml (¾ fl oz) **gin**
22 ml (¾ fl oz) **lemon juice**
22 ml (¾ fl oz) **Cocchi
  Americano**
15 ml (½ fl oz) **triple sec**
7 ml (¼ fl oz) **sugar syrup**
3 dashes **absinthe**
lemon twist, to garnish

Add all ingredients to a shaker
with ice. Shake and strain
into a frozen cocktail glass.
Garnish with a lemon twist.

BREAKFAST JULEP

60 ml (2 fl oz) **bourbon**
22 ml (¾ fl oz) **marmalade
  syrup**
small handful mint leaves
3 mint sprigs, to garnish

Add all ingredients to a julep
cup and mix well. Add crushed
ice and swizzle. Top up with
crushed ice and garnish
with mint sprigs.

MORNING GLORY FIZZ

60 ml (2 fl oz) **Scotch whisky**
22 ml (¾ fl oz) **lemon juice**
22 ml (¾ fl oz) **sugar syrup**
2 dashes **absinthe**
1 fresh egg white
soda
star anise, to garnish

Add all ingredients except egg
white and soda to a shaker.
Add the egg white and dry shake
to emulsify. Add ice and shake
hard. Strain into a frozen fizz

*The inventor of this drink,
Harry Craddock of the Savoy
Hotel in London, said three of
these in quick succession shall
revive a corpse!*

*Like this? Why not try the Odd
McIntyre? Just swap the gin
for Cognac.*

*Fancy it with gin? This one's
called the London Buck.*

*Or even sloe gin? That one's the
Cloudy Sky.*

*Scotch whisky more your style?
We call that the Presbyterian.*

*Make it a rye base and you've
got yourself a Cablegram.*

*For something a little special
that's guaranteed to get you
where you're going, switch
rum for gin once again and
add 15 ml (½ fl oz) of Fernet-
Branca. This cocktail is
aptly named the Late Night
Reviver, and it does exactly
what it says on the tin!*

*Feeling floral? How about the
Palma Fizz? This one swaps
rum for vodka and is finished
off with a spritz of rosewater.
Divine.*

*An alternative stiff start to the
morning … One of Sasha's
favourite jobs was separating
all the perfect star anise from
the broken ones. It really is all
in the details!*

*Don't like drinks with egg
white? No problem. Feel free
to leave it out, as well as the
soda, and simply serve this
cocktail up, in a frozen cocktail
glass instead.*

glass and top with soda. Garnish
with a perfect pod of star anise.

DARK & STORMY

If The Everleigh family had a
crest, it would have one of these
on it.

45 ml (1½ fl oz) **Gosling's Black
  Seal rum**
15 ml (½ fl oz) **lime juice**
22 ml (¾ fl oz) **ginger syrup**
soda
crystallised ginger, to garnish

Add all ingredients except soda
to a shaker with a tiny piece
of ice and whip. Pour into a
frozen Collins glass with ice and
top with soda. Garnish with
some crystallised ginger on a
toothpick.

FOG CUTTER

15 ml (½ fl oz) **light rum**
22 ml (¾ fl oz) **Cognac**
15 ml (½ fl oz) **gin**
15 ml (½ fl oz) **lemon juice**
22 ml (¾ fl oz) **orange juice**
15 ml (½ fl oz) **orgeat**
7 ml (¼ fl oz) **cream sherry**
mint sprig, to garnish

Add all ingredients to a shaker
with ice. Shake and strain into a
frozen double rocks glass with
ice. Float a little dash of cream
sherry on the top – just in case
you were worried you hadn't put
enough booze in. Garnish with a
large fragrant mint sprig.

MARMALADE COCKTAIL

SIMILAR BUT DIFFERENT

ABOUT THE AUTHORS

Michael Madrusan & Zara Young

Michael Madrusan is the founder of The Everleigh and The Elk Room, a golden-era cocktail bar overlooking Melbourne's Gertrude Street, Fitzroy.

The Everleigh, which opened on 4th July 2011, was named Bar of the Year by *Gourmet Traveller* in 2013, *Time Out*'s Cocktail Bar of the Year 2014, Bar of the Year 2015 and Cocktail Bar of the Year 2016. The Everleigh has also placed in the highly coveted *Drinks International*'s World's 50 Best Bars list 2013, 2014 and 2015.

Michael spent many years bartending in London and New York before returning home to Australia to open the country's first and only outpost of the Milk & Honey family. He has worked in some of the most revered bars in the world, including New York's Milk & Honey, Little Branch and PDT.

In October 2013, Zara Young left London to join The Everleigh and began working alongside Michael in the growth of The Everleigh family.

In January 2015, The Everleigh launched Navy Strength Ice Co., Australia's first hand-cut ice company, supplying Melbourne's bars and restaurants with crystal clear spears and blocks.

In May 2015 The Everleigh Bottling Co. was introduced, offering beautifully packaged ready-to-drink classic cocktails to stores, hotels, restaurants and bars across Australia.

In August 2015, Michael opened his second venue, Heartbreaker, in Melbourne's CBD. Inspired by the classic, much-loved bars of Los Angeles, this good-time bar pumps out classic rock and great booze until the early hours.

Michael was included in *The Age*'s Top 100 Most Influential People of 2012 and nominated for International Bartender of the Year at Tales of the Cocktail, New Orleans 2012.

ACKNOWLEDGEMENTS

We both have so many people to thank for the support and encouragement that allowed us to create this book.

Needless to say we wouldn't have been able to do any of this without the love and support of our families, near and far. Thanks to Bernadette for trusting that it was the right decision for her daughter to move to the other side of the world. To our beautiful sister Deanie whose strength has been a lighthouse in the roughest of storms, and to Greg for fixing so much more than just the furniture. To Gina and Stu for their advice, patience and 6 am wake up calls, the driving force behind it all. Neither of the bars would be here today without you. Thanks also to Johnny Madrusan, Mick and Em Smith, Linz and Ana for their help during The Everleigh build and to Anna Dunn for feeding us while we worked. To Adam Reid, my dear friend for putting together the most beautiful bar in the world with the help of his father, Dave. Thanks and love to my grandmother, Connie for always making the trip from Newcastle so she never misses anything we do. Thanks to our little buddy Frank whose whiny meows help us remember what's really important at the end of a long day.

Profound gratitude and respect to my best mates Mickey, Sammy, Ricey and the boys at Attaboy. Thanks to Jesse Genovese for all the LA times that have been influential to our endeavours. To Eric Alperin for his sound advice during the early stages of starting Navy Strength. To Alex Day, the reason I started the Cocktail Branches and his ongoing help with the smart stuff. To Andrew Thomason (Tomo) who left us in 2006 and is dearly missed. Thanks to Sasha for being my mentor and for giving us a job we can all be proud to tell our folks about.

Special thanks go to loyal Everleigh regulars, confidants and friends Chris and Kym whose beautiful Healesville hideaway home gave us the space and tranquillity to begin the writing process. Thank you to all those who love The Everleigh as much as we do; to all our regulars past and present. A big thanks to Tamil Rogeon for always bringing the noise. Thank you to Ted, Tom and Tim for their Friday ritual, Scott and Nicole for their Saturday ritual and the Ciciulla family for their dedication to taking a family photo on the The Everleigh stairs every time they visit without fail.

Huge thanks to Seb Raeburn for his tireless support and advice. To Cass and Leo of the Gertrude Hotel for always helping at a moment's notice, and neighbouring Gertrude Street venues for their support. A shout out to all bar owners who put their money where their mouth is, taking epic risks driven by a passion for this industry. Thank you to all the individuals who strive for, and achieve excellence and growth within this industry – those with integrity and humility over ego. Thanks to Melbourne as a city for its unwavering support and ability to embrace the new and exciting. This is a professional industry that deserves notable credit.

Thanks and cheers to The Everleigh team, past and present and to our naughty little siblings, team Heartbreaker. Special thanks to Marty for putting up with our crap and holding down the fort, and to Alastair Walker, my right-hand man from day one. Thanks to Joseph Schwartz, Lauren Schell, our sister bars and close friends across the pond.

We're ever grateful for the continued support of Michael Harden, Nick Shelton, Pat Nourse, Mike Rodriguez, Dave Kerr and Fiona Brook and the backing of *The Age*, *Broadsheet*, *Gourmet Traveller*, *Time Out*, *Drinks International*, San Antonio Cocktail Conference and Tales of the Cocktail.

Thank you to Dave Wondrich whose research has enriched our industry so significantly. Similarly to Jim Meehan and Robert Simonson.

Finally, a huge thanks to Thom and Kris for capturing the essence of The Everleigh in their beautiful photos. Thank you to Chris at Double Monk for allowing us to use your fabulous shoes and store. Thank you to Rhys, Claire, Monica and the rest of the TCYK team for designing such an exquisite book. Ultimately, thanks go to the team at Hardie Grant, Jane, Andrea and Vaughan for believing in us both and for making our dream a reality.

A Spot at the Bar

Authors:
Michael Madrusan & Zara Young

Publishing Director:
Jane Willson

Project Editor:
Andrea O'Connor

Editor:
Vanessa Lanaway

Design:
The Company You Keep

Creative Direction:
Rhys Gorgol

Designer:
Claire Bradbury

Photographers:
Kristoffer Paulsen
Thom Rigney

Illustrator:
Adam Nickel

Design Manager:
Vaughan Mossop

Production Manager:
Todd Rechner

Colour Reproduction:
Splitting Image Colour Studio

Printed in China by
1010 Printing International Ltd.

Hardie Grant Books would like to acknowledge the use
of various items of ephemera from The Waldorf Astoria
(New York), Bar Hemingway, The Ritz (Paris), Arthur
Schiller & Co. (Chicago), Keens Steakhouse (New
York), The Dorchester (London), Pabst Blue Ribbon
Beer (Milwaukee), Milk & Honey (New York), Trader
Vic's, Fisher & Hughes, Inc. (New Jersey), The St Regis
(Paris), Harvey's (New York), Stork Club (New York),
Little Branch (New York) and The Savoy (London).

Published in 2016 by Hardie Grant Books,
an imprint of Hardie Grant Publishing

A Cataloguing-in-Publication entry is
available from the catalogue of the National
Library of Australia at www.nla.gov.au.

A Spot at the Bar
ISBN 978 1 74379 131 8

Hardie Grant Books (Melbourne)
Building 1, 658 Church Street
Richmond, Victoria 3121
hardiegrantbooks.com.au

Hardie Grant Books (London)
5th & 6th Floors
52–54 Southwark Street
London SE1 1UN
hardiegrantbooks.co.uk